THE GRAND DESIGN—IV
Reflections of a soul/oversoul

THE GRAND DESIGN—IV
Reflections of a soul/oversoul

by

Patrick Francis

Auricle Enterprises Ltd

ISBN 0-9525509-3-8

Typessetting by STF, Celbridge, Co. Kildare, Ireland.
Printed by Colour Books, Baldoyle, Dublin 13, Ireland.

Contents

PART I

The Grand Design 1 6

Preface 7

Special relationships 13

Shame 15

Marriage 17

Time and space in relation to guides 21

Control: Communication 25

Abuse 31

Forgiveness 35

Reality 39

How best to deal with death 41

Mission/purpose v. free will 45

Akashic records? 47

Deservability 51

Sexual energy in the new consciousness 53

Money 57

Auras, etc. 61

Beings from other planets? 65

Imagination 67

PART II

What is life on planet earth going to be like in the future? 71

Conclusion 99

Transformation 100

Appendix: The Cathar Prophecy of 1244 A.D. 101

The Grand Design I

A book, so says the Author, with ideas
conflicting with orthodoxy,
and yet such ideas can hardly be put
into words.
And it seems that the conflict
does not exist at all,
But that all melts into a great sense
of what is.
The details, somehow though seeming
to conflict,
merge into a softness where I feel at home.
    Angels — or guides
    Evil   — or human weakness
    God   — or love
Perhaps it is the terminology which
fragments
And the journey to unity transcends
definition.
All we can do is to allow ourselves
to flow with the mystery
guided and guarded by the
Spirit of Light.

Jane Dowling

Reproduced by kind permission of the author

Preface

This is the fourth book in the series of books which I'm writing, I believe, in association with a spirit being known to me as Shebaka. I have explained in some detail in the prefaces to the earlier books, particularly the third one, how I came to write the books, so I won't go into all that again here.

On the whole, I found this a difficult book to write. I'm sure there are many different forms of what has come to be called channelling (an appropriate word, I think). It certainly doesn't come in a straightforward way for me. Sometimes it flows easily, and other times I have spent literally hours getting one paragraph done. I'm sure you know the sort of thing that comes into your head and you can't explain it because when you try to put words on it you lose the sense of it.

This book is rather like the first one for me in a way. As I indicated in the preface to that book, I was very hesitant about publishing it. It's not that I'm in any way doubtful about the material in this book but that I feel it somehow goes out on a limb, as the first one did — I still want (I think!) a quiet, anonymous life, although that possibility seems to be receding from me somewhat. No matter, I'll let it all unfold.

I keep being reminded of an Irish legend going back some two thousand years or so. It's about Oisin, who was one of the heroic Fianna, whose leader, and Oisin's father, was Fionn Mac Cumhail. A beautiful woman, riding a magnificent white steed, arrived one day to visit the Fianna. Her name was Niamh, and she became known as Niamh Cinn Oir — Niamh of the golden hair (head, literally). She had come to take Oisin with her to her country, which was called Tir na nOg — the land of (eternal) youth; she warned him, though, that he would never be able to go back to his own country. Oisin loved Niamh and decided to go with her on her white steed, although he was very sad about leaving his comrades.

Some hundreds of years passed, during which Oisin was blissfully happy with Niamh, but he still missed his friends very much. From time to time he pleaded with Niamh to help him go back for a brief trip. She told him that things would not be as they were when he was there, that all his comrades were long since gone, but he felt he had to go, and eventually she said that the white steed would take him, but that on no account was he to touch the ground or he'd never be able to get back to her. He promised, and soon he was back in Ireland — but, as Niamh had told him, it was all changed. There was no sign of his comrades. The people all seemed tiny. He saw about a dozen men trying to lift a big rock, to no avail. He, sitting, youthful, majestic, on the white steed, watched them, bemused, for some time, but, eventually, his patience ran out; he nudged the white steed up close to the rock, bent down, lifted the rock with one arm and threw it from him. In leaning down, however, he slipped from the back of the steed and was immediately transformed into an old man, barely able to move; the white steed vanished. There Oisin sat and lamented the loss of Niamh, the passing of the glories of the Fianna, the heroic times that he had enjoyed with them, and how the land was now peopled by pygmies.

Why I find the story particularly fascinating is that it seems to me to symbolise in some way the fall from the romance, the glory, the strength, the beauty, the eternal youth, of awareness, into the desolation, the weakness, the infirmity, the restrictiveness, of the unaware state; and how people allowed themselves to burrow into an acceptance of limitation. I hope that the vision of potential life on earth that's presented in the second part of this book may, at least, provide a stimulus towards the realisation of, if not Tir na nOg, whatever one's dream of utopia, or a heavenly state of being, might be.

Some time ago I was given a copy of a document entitled "The Cathar Prophecy of 1244 A.D.," which I have included as an appendix to this book. The Cathars seem to have been present in France only. They were condemned as heretics and were harshly persecuted with, apparently, the last of them having been burnt at the stake by the Inquisition at Montsegur, Languedoc, in 1244. They left the prophecy that what they called the church of love would be proclaimed in 1986. The philosophy outlined in the prophecy seems to me to be very relevant to what's happening in the present shifting of consciousness. In any case, I want to pay tribute to the courage of largely forgotten victims of some of the many cruelties that dogmatic people have, through the ages, inflicted on those who professed beliefs differing from theirs.

Once again I have to apologise to any readers who may be offended by my using 'he' instead of 'he/she'. I have come across books written with 'he' and 'she' being interchanged in separate sections, but that device seemed to me to disrupt the flow of the material. I tried using 'he/she' but I thought it was inelegant and unwieldy, so for the sake of consistency and easy reading I decided to continue as I had started. Thanks for your understanding.

Patrick Francis

January, 1995.

Part I

Special Relationships

26th March — 9th April, 1993: While we don't break the continuity of our association by saying hellos and goodbyes, still it seems auspicious to me to greet the start of our fourth book with a joyful note of welcome and love from all of us involved in this project to you and all our readers, the number of whom, I'm happy to see, is growing steadily. Our love surrounds you all always.

I'd like to consider in our opening session how individuality fits in with oneness, or non-separation, and to expand our exploration into how, or whether, special relationships are consistent with oneness. By oneness I mean, of course, oneness with God/love/feeling and all its expressions.

The fundamental starting point in our consideration has to be that nothing exists outside of God; all is God, God is all, whatever way one likes to put it. Accordingly, as God is in each one of us, we are all linked together in God. In that sense we are all one. How, then, is there individuality?

Suppose we take an example of cars. There are all sorts of designs of cars, with vast differences between them. Yet they all have one thing in common — they cannot operate — in other words, they have no life — without a supply of energy.

The God within us is the supply of energy that animates us. It's an unfailing, unending source of supply no matter what transitional forms our evolutionary journeys involve.

The love that is God does not have to express itself in any particular pattern; it evolves in whatever way it wishes. Expression into individual parts was (is) inherent in that evolution. While all the individual parts are animated by God and are thus inextricably linked to each other, each part is, nonetheless, completely individualistic, literally a universe in itself.

The more aware souls become, the more they express the love (God) that they are. It becomes easier to love unconditionally because it becomes easier to look behind the defensive masks with which souls seek to cloak their vulnerability. The lovableness of each soul becomes more readily apparent.

If the aware soul, then, loves every other soul, does a hungering for special relationships reflect a lack of awareness? No. Love is of its nature expansive. The more aware a soul is, the more it wishes to spread itself, to let its loving expression know no frontiers.

The expression of God into individual parts enabled special affinities between souls. The notion of God as an entity without a variety of individual expression is one of stagnation which is not consistent with evolving consciousness. The ultimate return to full awareness of souls still on that path will not result in a loss of individuality into a merging with a Source (God). (There wouldn't be much fun in a soul communicating indefinitely with itself!)

Full awareness means an unconditionally loving relationship with all souls (oversouls). Within that, there are special affinities which cover a wide range of souls. And, within the ambit of the special affinities, there are what are commonly called soul mates — wonderfully intimate relationships between two souls. Every soul (oversoul) has a soul mate. There comes a time — or times — when souls are ready consciously to meet their soul mates while they are both in human form. That is possible within the ultimate context of oneness and when it happens the love for all others of the particular people is enhanced by the unlimited nature of their love for each other.

Shame

4th July: Consider an infant. It lives through its feelings, doesn't it? (I'm deliberately using "it" rather than "he/she" because sex distinction has no relevance for an infant.) It gurgles, it cries, it smiles, it kicks its feet, it expresses its feelings exactly as they are. It has no fear, its sense of wonder is boundless, everything is possible, even (in some countries) the notion of Santa Claus coming down every chimney in the whole world at the same time on the one night. But with the passage of time it begins to be influenced by its environment. Its parents'/guardians' belief systems introduce controlling factors. Later on, other environmental influences, such as, schools, teachers, peer groups, also contribute towards establishing a particular pattern of thinking in the emerging child, adolescent, adult — so that the feeling infant is submerged in the rational man/woman.

A constant theme running through our sessions is the necessity for each soul to free itself from conditioning. One of the strongest ingredients in conditioning is shame.

What is shame? A common definition would probably be that it is a feeling induced by guilt, or dishonour, or going against customary behaviour in some way. But, in my view, shame has nothing at all to do with feelings; it's a conditioned pattern of thinking which imposes itself on feelings and thus creates emotions, or unaware expressions of feelings. An infant, or a very young child, doesn't feel ashamed of, for example, its nakedness, or of how it behaves. It only learns to be ashamed of such things because its experiences in growing up teaches it to think that way.

Life on earth is governed by rules and regulations. Each nation/state, each society, each religion, determines its own laws, its own rules for living under its ambit of control. The person who offends against those rules, who "sins", is expected to feel ashamed of his behaviour. If he persists in offending, he is locked away in some institution, or tolerated as somebody who is not "normal", or, perhaps, exceptionally, as somebody who has established such a position of independence that he is outside the "norm", a "character" in his own right.

Sources of shame are extensive. Examples may be:- poverty, illegitimacy, nakedness, unemployment, adultery, infidelity, sexual practices, impotence, disability, parents, children, accents, skin colour, overweight, alcoholism, drug-taking, incontinence, sexual performance, illiteracy, childlessness, promiscuity, virginity, failure to pass examinations or to succeed at interviews for jobs or promotions, work, level of pay, living accommodation, physical appearance, inability to compete, desertion, bankruptcy, imprisonment, relatives, social status. What all the sources have in common is that their origins derive from the ashamed person's perception of the behaviour expected from him by another/others, or his own position within the society in which he lives; in other words, he is controlled by what he thinks about himself and/or what he thinks another/others think about him.

How does one become free of shame, or possible occasions of shame? Firstly, by accepting that the source of shame is thought, the conditioned pattern of thinking that has imprisoned the child growing into adulthood, and, secondly, by letting go of that conditioned pattern of thinking and learning to trust feelings (as distinct from emotions, such as, anger, jealousy, lust, possessiveness). Where feelings are concerned there are no absolutes, no right or wrong, no good or bad, or, put another way, feelings are the only absolute because they make no judgement, they just are. Judgement intrudes when thoughts take over because thoughts eventually categorise, they only know what they know, which is always limited. There's a lot of progress in being able to say *I know that I don't know.*

Shame is a product of a lack of self-acceptance, including, of course, acceptance of one's body. Your body (as everybody's) is the vehicle which you have chosen to fulfil your purpose on earth. It is ideally suited to that purpose. As and when you accept fully (through feelings as well as thought) that you are divine consciousness, that God is within, and as you align yourself with that consciousness, it will be impossible for you to be ashamed of yourself. Divine consciousness does not know shame.

Marriage

10th-29th December: I'm talking about marriage in the context of a union between a man and a woman, which is given a legal standing, and sometimes a sacramental standing, within communities and national groupings.

Conventional expectation is that partners within a marriage are sexually faithful to each other and do not consider other liaisons.

Societies are built around marriages and nation/states around societies. The ideal is that a harmonious family home is a secure base for the birth and upbringing of children and for the maintenance of order within communities.

If the possibility of reincarnation is accepted, it is likely, of course, that an individual soul will have, and have had, many different relationships, some of them resulting in marriage. It follows that there can be no such thing as marriage in an exclusive sense, i.e., that a married couple are bound to each other for all eternity. They may wish to have a continuity of relationship, but there's no compulsion in it, no mandatory divine law; there couldn't be, of course, given the existence of free will.

Needless to say, I want to examine the concept of marriage from a spiritual point of view rather than from any standpoint of its convenience as a regulatory form within society.

Marriage, as such, has no special significance in so far as expression of spirituality is concerned. Relationships, including relationships within marriage, do have, of course, great spiritual importance, both in the sense of general contact with the people in one's world and, also, in more intimate contact with a special other, or others. A person can present a front to the world in general and hide behind an image that he has created for himself, but if he wants to achieve an intimate relationship with another person he will have to let go of his defensive barriers and reveal himself as he is, which includes acknowledging his vulnerability; otherwise the relationship will be artificial.

Marriage, or a marriage-type relationship, brings together two people in a situation where intimacy has to feature in some way. It is essential that at some stage in its evolution a soul should be able to reach a state of total intimacy with another soul and that this should be done within a climate of complete freedom, i.e., with no suppression of personality, no possessiveness, no strings of any kind. Marriage-type relationships allow for that possibility, although, in practice, of course, the interaction of energies within those relationships often causes much conflict, sometimes to such an extent that living together may no longer be spiritually desirable.

It's not possible for me to discuss marriage without putting it into a reincarnational context. The grand design envisaged a vast variety of possibilities whereby souls would get opportunities for growth in awareness; how they availed, or would avail, themselves of those opportunities depended on their use of free will. In their human manifestations people have continually created effects through their use of free will in their interaction with people which have put them into positions of karmic obligation towards those people. Subsequent relationships between them are designed to clear those obligations. Sometimes, unfortunately, the obligations are deepened rather than lessened, and thus an apparently never-ending cycle of reincarnational involvement seems to exist and the realisation of a state of intimacy in relationship recedes into increasing desperation.

As I have intimated in earlier sessions, the grand design moved into a new phase in recent years; an integral part of that phase is the emphasis on guides and how they can help people who are still in the second stage of evolutionary growth to release themselves from the effects of their use of free will, without at the same time interfering with their free will. The fundamental starting point is that people should accept their divinity, their unity with God, and that the acceptance should not just be intellectual but should also be in their feelings. It's not a question of doing anything, as such; it's simply letting a feeling happen, or letting go into a feeling. *(I outlined a way of letting the feeling happen on pages 73-75 of our third book.)* As the feeling of unity becomes a way of life, a person automatically fulfils his purpose as inevitably as a wave in the sea fulfils its purpose; there's no resistance to the flow (of life). For somebody who is aware enough to come to both an intellectual and a feeling acceptance of his divinity, it is likely, and more probably certain, that his purpose is to free himself completely from the wheel of karmic obligation, so that life on earth will have no more to offer him by way of learning experiences. (It will, of course, be open to him to choose to reincarnate in order to help others.)

A source of huge confusion for people on earth is that their conditioning links them to making judgements, including judgements on themselves, on happenings or events. I know I'm repeating myself when I say that happenings are of no importance in themselves; their importance lies in the effects that they create on people's feelings and thoughts. The happenings are over and done with (and are succeeded by other happenings) but their effects remain; and the extent of the effects depends on the sensitivity of the people experiencing them. (The same thing can happen to two different people but the effects on them will not be similar.)

The whole structure and functioning of planet earth is based on happenings, on things being done. In spirit, creation is instantaneous; a soul in spirit has only to feel and think about something and it *is*; whereas on earth feeling and thinking about something are not enough, although they are still the primary ingredients in creativity; something has to be done before there's a physical reality. It is understandable, then, that judgements are made on the basis of what people do rather than on what they feel or think. But it hardly requires deep consideration to see how artificial such judgements can be. Things are done for a multiplicity of reasons, some of which may be totally true to the feelings and thoughts behind them, but many of which are likely to be controlled by conditioned responses where the thoughts are in conflict with, and suppressing, the feelings. Nobody can vailidly make a judgement on the actions of another because no soul can enter another soul or know that soul's inner motivation.

In order, then, to be able to flow with life, to be more truly divine, a person needs to free himself from conditioning so that he can find purity in his motivation and not allow himself to be controlled by any judgemental thinking. His motivation is geared totally towards being himself, knowing that the more he can succeed in that aim, the more he will relate to his world, and the people in it, with an integrity of purpose. Embarking on that journey may be a source of revolution for him. He can no longer hide behind a mask of any kind. It's a difficult, often monumental, task to break away from many centuries of conditioning which has created its own form of security and resists with great intensity every step of the process of being let go.

I seem to have digressed somewhat from talking specifically about marriage into discussing conditioning in general. Marriage, though, is the most central vehicle of conditioning on planet earth. In saying earlier that to be more truly divine a person needs to free himself from conditioning I don't want to be taken as implying that marriage as an institution has no place in the grand design. I mentioned that in itself it has no special spiritual significance; but it serves to bring two people together into a relationship which provides them with an opportunity to come to terms with intimacy, with being more truly themselves. If they are not controlled by conditioning, e.g., what they think is expected of them, and if they can expand into an awareness, including a feeling, of their own divinity, partners in a marriage can be helped significantly in breaking the cycle of karmic obligation, although in the process they may temporarily find themselves in conflict with each other as well as with the institutional demands of the society in which they live. Ultimately, the object is that all relationships should be clear, i.e., not controlled by any strings, such as, duty, possessiveness, human respect, pride, security, and that all people should relate to each other in an unconditionally loving way.

Those souls who are now on earth and those who will be coming into earth from now on are being given greater opportunities than have ever before been present in the evolution of earth to free themselves from the reincarnational cycle. As I have said, it's a difficult task. However, there's no limit to the help available. All that's needed is not to be too proud to ask for it and to be willing to receive it.

Time and Space in Relation to Guides

4th - 10th January, 1994: A question put to you recently on which you'd like elucidation was — "How come time and space mean nothing to our spirit guides when they have probably evolved through human lifetimes?"

It's a fact that time and space, as you know them, are a feature of earth only. They are expressions of structure and, therefore, limitation. The world of spirit exists outside of structure and, accordingly, is unlimited in its expression.

Guides retain memories of earth and its structures and, of course, those memories help them in dealing with human beings. You might say that it's an ironic thing that souls come from the timelessness and spacelessness of spirit into physical bodies confined within the restrictiveness of time and space and that they have spirit guides who have themselves left that restrictiveness behind and yet see it as a positive thing that the human beings whom they are helping should be subject to the restrictiveness. You see, though, what the guides are doing is trying to help their temporarily human friends to reach more and more feeling of the freedom of spirit within the confined conditions of earth, and they can do that more effectively because they are free spirits themselves. One of the reasons why souls can gain considerable benefit from adopting human form is that they have allowed themselves to become limited by structured thinking, and by coming into that type of environment they are, ideally, brought up against the effects of such thinking, whereas in spirit, because vibrations don't mix in the same way as they do on earth (in spirit like tends to associate exclusively with like), they might continue to exist within an unchanging framework of thought indefinitely.

It's not that time and space mean nothing to guides, it's that they're not limited by their rigid structures, and that, as I've said already, they want to convey the feeling of their freedom of spirit to their human charges. At the same time, it's fair to say that, in being free themselves and in becoming accustomed to that way of being, it takes an effort for them to attune themselves to an environment that exists in such a structured way.

An illustration might be helpful. Suppose you hear about a community comprising a number of people who decided to "get away from it all", to establish a lifestyle for themselves where they would be totally free to do what they wanted to do, even if that meant doing nothing at all. They are in the fortunate position that they had in their younger years acquired enough money to be free of material worries. The only meaning that time has for them is that day passes into night and night into day. They have no clocks or calendars to mark the movement of time through days into weeks and months and years. They deliberately sought out and found a location where the climate allows them to live within houses or without them, as they wish. While they are still, as human beings, confined within physical formations, such as their own bodies, they have become accustomed to feelings of spacelessness — the sort of feeling that one gets from gazing at the vastness of the sea or the seemingly endless range of the sky. They are no longer controlled by the limitations of space.

Suppose that you feel that you'd like to sample that way of life. You understand that the community has no rules and regulations and does not apply any process of selectivity; it's open to you, or anybody else, to swell its numbers. You are completely free to come or go as you wish.

You join the community and the lifestyle suits you very well. Soon, (since you've lost track of time, you don't know how long), your previous way of life becomes gradually a hazy memory for you; you can still recall it, but you have moved into such a vastly different way that the details are shrouded in a mist of what is now an unreality for you.

Suppose that a colleague from your earlier life comes to visit you and starts discussing with you matters which previously would have been of gripping interest to you. Now, however, you find that you're seeing those matters in a totally different light and you approach the interaction with your former colleague both from his perspective in so far as you can now bring yourself to identify with it (and that identification is helped by your background knowledge) and also from the broader perspective of your present way. You still know about time and space as they are structured within his world, but they mean nothing to you in your life as it now is.

In using the above illustration, which is intended to convey that there may be circumstances even within the human condition where notions of time and space as commonly understood may have no meaning. I don't want to imply that an ideal way of living on earth would be to establish or join a community such as the one I have described. It may be, for some; it all depends on what souls wish to learn from their earth experiences. In fact, it is likely that for most souls participation in the experiences of earth, in all their restrictiveness, is the best way to achieve growth in consciousness.

Control: Communication

5th-29th May: In earlier sessions we have discussed different ways, including prayer, in which people seek to exercise control over others. In this session I want to explore more deeply means by which people can protect themselves from such control. I also want to look further into the whole question of communication, not alone communication with guides/oversouls, but also communication between souls in their interaction as humans and as spirit beings, both as between themselves as humans and between spirit beings and humans.

Souls in spirit often seek to control souls who are still in physical bodies. People don't miraculously change when they move from one state to another; somebody who is in the habit of exercising control over others while on earth will be likely to want to continue to do so after physical death. Accordingly, a human being may have to cope with controlling influences from spirit and physical sources.

The notion of possession figures in any consideration of control from a spirit source. I have gone into that at some length in previous sessions where I discounted completely even the remotest possibility of possession by way of a spirit being taking over a human's body. The only way that control can happen in the interaction between spirit and human beings is by intrusion into the human's aura or etheric body. In that case, the solution for the human being is to keep his aura clear. How can that be achieved?

In our first book I recommended that, if a person can accept that he has guides helping him, he should ask them to keep his aura clear from all negative energies. The guides cannot (in the sense that they may not) interfere with free will; it's not consistent with their state of awareness that they should do so. Requesting them for protection is an expression of free will and allows them freedom to surround their human charge with an impenetrable shield which is only lifted at his request. There's no need to keep on asking — once is enough.

If a person can't accept that he has guides helping him, or if he doesn't believe that they can provide the protection he needs, what can he do? He can regularly cleanse his aura by swirling motions of his hands around his body, using his third eye (centre of the forehead) as a base; or he can imagine himself as a cocoon of light coloured to his preference; or he can establish a regular pattern of meditation on unity with God/love; or he can free himself as far as possible from all fears, anxieties, tensions, worries, emotional pressures of any kind, through whatever form of relaxation suits him; or he can use whatever other ritual may appeal to him.

Surprisingly (!), in my view, the simplest and most effective way to keep one's aura clear is to ask one's guides to arrange it; there's no point in keeping them unemployed!

Now, suppose that there are some people who feel betrayed by some action or actions of yours and are thinking resentful thoughts about you. And suppose, also, that there are others who feel that you have gone astray somehow in the way you're living your life and are praying constantly that you'll "see the light" and rectify matters. In the first instance, there's a wave of resentful thoughts being directed at you; in the second, the thoughts may be caring, but, of course, the people who are directing them at you have made a judgement about you according to their own belief systems and are seeking to control you within those beliefs.

You may be completely unaware that any of those thoughts are being directed at you; or you may be marginally aware of them; or you may be aware of some of them; or, indeed, you may be fully aware of them.

Suppose, though, that, whether you are fully, or partly, or not at all, aware of them, your aura is unprotected, what effect is created on you? You'll find yourself being edgy, irritable perhaps, or depressed, or very tired, for no apparent reason, or feeling unwell, maybe, even, becoming quite ill. You'll be more vulnerable to infections and, in the longer term, your physical (and, perhaps, mental) health could be seriously damaged.

If you ask your guides to keep your aura clear, will that protect you from the effects of controlling thoughts being directed at you from all sources, i.e., physical and spirit sources? Most certainly, it will. If you're aware of those thoughts, or, even, suspect their existence, you may allow yourself to be affected by them, for example, by feeling defensive or rejected. It's your prerogative (privilege?) as a human being to allow your-self to be vulnerable. But of one thing you can be certain — no external influence will have power to interfere with your life purpose once you have given permission to your guides to keep your aura clear of any such interfering influences.

I cannot emphasise strongly enough how important it is that people should not set themselves up as judges of others. Prayer can be a most insidious form of judgement because it is seen as an act of piety; asking God to make a person see the error of his ways and do what's "right" is a stark example of negative controlling influence. Of course, if prayer is offered in a spirit of unconditional love, that can only be helpful; it's send-ing love in a totally free way.

Generally speaking, people have little or no realisation of the power of thought. As I have explained in earlier sessions, feeling is the source of creation and feeling concentrates itself in thought, which engineers and focuses action. Feelings are expansive, free-flowing; thoughts put struc-tures on them. Everything on earth is structured; all the physical world dis-tributes itself, or is distributed, into form of some kind. All physical cre-ation exists through concentration of feelings into thoughts on the part of its creators. When one considers the immensity of what has been created in physical terms, one can then perhaps more readily imagine the sheer force of concentrated thoughts directed by a person or groups of people towards another or others.

Language is not a factor in spirit in the same way as it is on earth. Communication between souls in spirit is rather like telepathy. It is not necessary to put thoughts into a language structure. In the world of spirit like associates with like. Accordingly, communication is easier. However, growth in consciousness may be much slower in spirit than on earth if souls are existing in a climate of closed-mindedness. Because earth is such a dense vibration, the possibility exists of many different levels of aware-ness interacting, which facilitates faster growth. A disadvantage is that communication has to be articulated — usually — and is, therefore, subject to misinterpretation.

Souls in spirit seeking to communicate with humans are handicapped by the fact that they are no longer operating within the forms, e.g., language, which they used on earth. At the same time, if they are to make themselves understood, they must find a way of communicating which will somehow fit in with the way of earth. It's an extremely sensitive business and cannot be achieved successfully without a lot of cooperation at the human end. Something has to be injected into the consciousness of the human recipient which he can seem to hear or see although it's not audible or visible in physical terms. Ideally, the human should be open-minded, tolerant, with no rigid beliefs, as well as being relaxed, patient and trusting. Being literal-minded or trying to see things in black and white terms is a disadvantage in receiving communication from spirit. It is important to learn to discriminate — souls are not infallible just because they happen to be in spirit.

How do you know whether you're receiving communication from a spirit source? How can you bring a certainty into it given that it's not possible for a soul in spirit to be present with you in the same way as a human friend would be? The simple answer is that you can't achieve the same type of certainty as you can in the physical world. I should say the certainy that you may think you have, because there's no certainty in any continuing sense in the physical world, since every body dies and everything else disintegrates. In the long run, the only continuity is in your feelings and thoughts which constitute your consciousness. So the real world for each and every soul is an internal one created by its feelings and thoughts. That world is outside of time and space and, accordingly, is in a permanent state of connectedness in some form with all other individual worlds and with the universe as a whole. Ultimately, therefore, the certainty that you think you have in physical evidence is only an illusion, whereas the reality — what you are when you forego all your material possessions, including your body — is your state of mind/soul, which is linked, consciously or unconsciously, with all other souls.

If, then, the reality is soul-to-soul communication, why is it so difficult to establish more clear links between spirit and human beings? I already mentioned the difference between the forms of communication, e.g., language structures, on earth as opposed to telepathic intercourse in spirit. The vast difference in vibrations — the heavy, dense vibration of earth in contrast with the light vibration of spirit — also impedes communication. There are other factors, such as the readiness and capacity of both spirit and human beings to establish links. Ultimately, however, the challenge for humans is to learn to trust. The human condition exists because souls lost their awareness of themselves, their divine selves. In seeking to regain that awareness they *must* sometime, somehow, let go of all conditioning, look beyond the narrow confines of the physical world, still the cacophony of energy-sapping thoughts endlessly creating mountains out of molehills, and, in a state of relaxation, trust the insights that, helped by their guides, constantly flow through to them from their linking in with the infinity of consciousness. Shifts in consciousness don't happen unless people are prepared to take risks to develop their intuitive abilities. The rewards are unlimited; literally, the reattainment of the kingdom of heaven within them, or, put another way, letting God happen in them.

Abuse

1st May - 26th June: One of the features of the evolution of life on earth has been the proliferation of therapies aimed at helping people deal with causes or sources of perceived dysfunctionalism, rather than symptoms. The acceleration of growth in consciousness, particularly in the latter part of this century, has, of course, been at the root of that trend.

In earlier times there was a prevailing view that more harm than good could come out of delving too deeply into the whys and wherefores. In that way people could get on with their lives and make the best of whatever fate or a higher power had in store for them. The stones were better left unturned as there was no telling where the worms would go! As so much of earlier conditioning had the effect of making people feel like worms (the worms won't take offence, I hope, since they'll hardly be reading this — not in their present form, at least!) there was, perhaps, more shelter under the stones anyway.

What's the answer? Is it helpful to delve into past experiences in order to heal present conditions? Or is it desirable to forget about the past and get on with life as it is?

If we conclude that delving into the past is a helpful proposition, the question arises as to what constitutes the past. Is it to be understood as the present life, or all past lives as well as the present life, or selected past lives in conjunction with the present life? If it is accepted that reincarnation, or the possibility of reincarnation, is a fact, then it has to follow that the effects of past life happenings are carried through emotionally into the present life. Yet, generally speaking, people don't remember their past lives and, if they don't, aren't conclusions based on examination of the present life and the effects of its happenings necessarily flawed since there isn't access to enough factual information on which to make judgements? And then, although many people accept the possibility of reincarnation, many don't, and the many who don't include (some) therapists whose training predisposes them to disregard what is outside the boundaries of scientific proof.

Abuse in one form or another is a common feature of life on earth. Ideally, evolution is intended to operate in such a way that human beings will behave with greater awareness than animals. Unfortunately, the reverse is often the case. As a general rule, animals do not abuse each other. They kill each other, but, usually, for survival purposes only. To say that people who have acted cruelly towards others were/are like animals is a grave injustice to animals. It's a sad fact that the attainment of an awareness level sufficient to enable the operation of free will does not guarantee the exercise of free will in a manner that respects the dignity of all life forms.

Examples of abuse are manifold, such as, torture, both mental and physical, battering, rape, looting, theft, authoritarianism, brainwashing, bigotry, intolerance, direct and indirect forms of control, criticism, fear, slander, starvation, slave wages, sarcasm, miserliness, political manipulation, incest, favouritism in, say, family/employee situations, addiction to drugs/alcohol, sexual harassment, possessiveness. A particularly horrific form of abuse is the rape of children.

Within the many possibilities of abuse that exist it is difficult for any person — impossible, I should say — to avoid being an abuser and/or a victim at some stages in their lives. In this session, I'd like to concentrate our consideration on the area of sexual abuse, not sexual abuse in general but sexual abuse of children in particular.

There can be no doubt that some children are sexually abused. Girls are predominantly the victims and relatives or guardians usually the perpetrators. Sometimes the victims remember the abuse clearly, sometimes they have only a feeling of it, and sometimes they may block out the memory of it altogether as the only way they can get on with living their lives.

My special concern in this session is about cases where there's no clear memory of sexual abuse. Suppose a woman, due to circumstances in her life, decides that she needs therapy. In the unfolding of the interaction with her therapist her childhood relationships are explored. Obviously, her relationship with her parents cannot but have had significant influences on her conditioning, including her sexual expression. Her feelings about each of her parents are examined. Generally, there was a reticence about sexual matters in so far as both her parents were concerned. She remembers being cuddled by her father, but, at a certain stage, when she was about nine, he no longer made any physical demonstrations of love towards her. For some time she continued to put her arms around his neck or to attempt to sit on his lap but either he pushed her away or her mother gave her something to do to distract her. Soon she got the message.

In the course of the therapy the possible reasons for the behavioural change on her father's part and also her mother's obvious discouragement of any physical contact between father and daughter are analysed. A possible explanation could be that her father's cuddling of her was more sexual than parental; that her mother became aware of that and made sure it stopped. That explanation would help to make sense of some of the problems that she has been experiencing in her adult life. However, since she has no memory of anything that might be construed as sexual abuse, how can she find proof of something which is now, to her thinking, moving more into the realms of probability than possibility? An obvious answer is to confront her parents, who are both still alive. She does so. They are horrified and deeply disturbed, and vehemently deny any suggestion of sexual abuse. The resulting situation is that there's now a deep rift in the relationship between parents and daughter.

The question arises as to whether the woman's last situation is now worse than her first. It undoubtedly is, in my view, because she has transferred responsibility from herself to her parents and she will never be able to heal herself without taking responsibility for herself.

I don't want to be taken as devaluing therapy in any way. However, therapists are also human and are limited by their own conditioning. In many cases the notion of past sexual abuse has proved to be too convenient a solution for present perceived problems.

It may well be that, in exploring childhood and adolescent experiences of a present life, impressions of a previous life, or more than one life, filter through to the surface of one's consciousness, and if there's no awareness or acceptance of such a possibility it is, I think, easy to see how those impressions could be superimposed on the experiences and relationships of the present life — with resultant havoc. Another possibility is that, say, a particularly sensitive girl will be responsive to sexual tensions between her parents with consequential confusing emotions within herself; a subtle form of abuse which has no physical manifestation.

What I'm attempting to convey in this session is that reaching conclusions from projected and incidentally limited perspectives is, at best, unwise and, at worst, dangerous. All forms of psychiatric, psychological, counselling evaluations need to expand their horizons. In spite of the recent acceleration of growth in consciousness, which is momentously significant and encouraging, humanity, in general, is still in an embryonic state struggling to come to terms with its divinity; as it does, its understanding will automatically increase so that it won't seek to jump to conclusions which may be totally unwarranted and unjust invasions of privacy.

You may ask why is it that, if people carry with them effects from past lives which influence their present lives, the grand design does not provide for even selective memory recall of past life experiences which would be relevant to the present life and assist in understanding it. The notion of reincarnation is offensive to the beliefs of many people and expansion of their beliefs can only come through their free will. For those who believe in reincarnation, or the possibility of it, there's a matter of timing — in other words, the stage of being ready to hear and accept the information. The grand design ensures that people who are open to receive will always be guided to the appropriate sources of help for them.

There are, of course, many instances where people consciously remember having been sexually abused as children in their present lives. I propose to include consideration of such cases in our next session.

Forgiveness

27th-30th June: According to some of your religious beliefs, all human beings are born in sin and are only cleansed of their sins and forgiven by God through the sacrament of baptism. Religious ceremonies invariably incorporate prayers for God's forgiveness of sins.

If you feel that somebody has hurt you, rejected you, done you an injustice of some kind, does that mean that at some stage you must forgive that person? Is it, indeed, open to you to forgive? Is there, in fact, anything to forgive?

Everybody in the human condition has felt hurt or abandoned or rejected or betrayed, many times perhaps, in their evolution. Occasions of hurt, etc., are present in daily human interaction — a perceived critical word or look, for example, can be a source of considerable hurt to a highly sensitive person. The more sensitive one is, the more likely one is to be open to hurt. Often the person who is deemed to be responsible for causing hurt is quite unconscious of that.

Emotional hurt in its different manifestations — rejection, abandonment, etc., — is subjective. What causes hurt to one person will have no effect on another. It follows, then, that people are hurt according to their capacity to receive hurt — or, put another way, to the extent that they allow it.

Physical cruelty, of course, causes emotional as well as physical hurt. An obvious example of that is sexual abuse. For instance, how can a child avoid being hurt, or not allow itself to be hurt, by an abusing parent or adult?

I think it's a reasonable conclusion that in some in some instances hurt is unavoidable in the human condition. The more a person reaches self-acceptance and a feeling of oneness with God in him, the less possibility there is of his being hurt — his capacity to receive hurt is diminishing in accordance with his increasing feeling of oneness with God.

Even though it's true, then, that he is only hurt who allows that to happen, it is humanly a fact that nobody who has ever come on earth, no matter how evolved, has avoided being hurt. So consideration of the question of forgiveness is relevant.

What does forgiveness mean? It may be helpful to use an illustration.

As a child, Helen was sexually abused by her father. In later life there's no question of her being in any doubt about that — she remembers it vividly. She was a young child when it started — only five years of age — and it continued intermittently for several years. Her father had warned her not to tell anybody, that it was their secret. Helen loved her father. His approval was very important to her. She had not yet learned what would generally be regarded as acceptable behaviour in terms of sexual morality within the particular environment into which she was born. In the earlier stages, the physical pain and discomfort caused by the sexual acts were cushioned by the conspiratorial closeness of her relationship with her father and by the specially favoured status which she enjoyed with him.

As she grew older, however, and as she developed into conformity with her environment, Helen became more and more uncomfortable about the situation with her father. She didn't want to risk losing his approval, but she was increasingly in a state of emotional confusion and the secrecy had become a burden of guilt rather than a special feeling of closeness.

Helen's father died when she was ten. His death, which was sudden, deeply shocked her, but, at least, it put an end to the continuing physical situation. The emotional trauma, however, remained with her and affected her in her subsequent adult relationships, particularly where her sexual expression was concerned. For years she suppressed as best she could the memory of the whole situation, including the memory of her father, but now she has come to a stage where she feels she'll have to come to terms with it.

Understandably, Helen feels very bitter and angry about the circumstances of her childhood and, in particular, about her father, who was in a position of control over those circumstances. Eventually, however, for her own protection, she will need to transform those emotions into feelings of forgiveness. The question, then, is — forgiveness of whom? An obvious answer is her father, since he was the controller of the situation. But that isn't the answer. What she really needs to do is to forgive herself; that's where freedom for her lies.

You may well ask — how could that be the answer when she was entirely blameless in her childhood innocence? She was, indeed, blameless but she took on a heavy burden of guilt which conditioned her into a deep lack of self-acceptance. Accordingly, in her self-expression she was not free to be truly herself. In a sense, she punished herself for having been a victim.

In an earlier session (in our third book) I said that each soul can only take responsibility for itself. Since you agonised over the use of the word 'can' and wondered whether you were misinterpreting what was coming through to you, I elaborated to the effect that a soul "*cannot* deny any other soul the right to take responsibility for itself. It's not a matter of choice; the possibility doesn't exist within the expression of God/love."

It may seem strange to say that if Helen feels that she has to forgive her father she's taking responsibility for him. Yet, that's what she would be doing. Her father's motivation in his dealings with her is something for which only he can take responsibility. Certainly, his actions had a profound effect on Helen. The effect remained long after the actions ceased. But Helen must also take responsibility for herself. She was a child, physically powerless to prevent herself from being a victim of abuse by somebody who was in a special position of trust in relation to her, but now she's an adult still controlled by the effects of the abuse. The effects are there in the way she is in herself, how she feels and thinks. That's how she creates her universe. Nobody can control how she feels and thinks unless she allows that to happen. The scope of her actions may be controllable but not her feelings and thoughts. So, if she forgives herself for taking on whatever burden (guilt, etc.,) has affected her self-acceptance, she is giving herself freedom to be herself without restriction.

If I may put the illustration into a broader perspective, Helen's journey as a soul seeking to regain the awareness which she had lost (as one of the "fallen angels" — the "1%", as explained in our first book) will have operated through many human expressions, some of which will, inevitably, have involved her as an abuser as well as a victim. It is a fact, however unpalatable it may be, that each soul chooses its parents and the environment into which it is born. In its own judgement of itself the soul is choosing experiences designed to deal with recurring effects of other experiences in its continuing evolutionary journey. The likelihood is that the pattern of its evolution is a constantly repeating cycle of experiences and conditioned responses to them; for example, an abuser in one life, a victim in another; it punishes itself for being an abuser (in some form) in one life by being a victim in another. The way of being a victim may not be directly linked with that of the abuser — e.g., a murderer in one lifetime may choose a different form of punishment, other than being murdered, in another lifetime.

It is important to stress that punishment is not imposed on any soul by any external source, such as a judgemental God; it is always self-imposed. Ultimately, the cycle of repeating patterns is only broken when the soul decides that it no longer needs to punish itself; in other words, when it allows itself to forgive itself for all its "sins" of unawareness.

All of us who were the fallen angels seriously transgressed against our own divinity — against God in us. But we couldn't negate that divinity, although, in the process of our transgression, we unawarely did our best to do so. Some of us have already forgiven ourselves for our presumption that we could achieve an impossibility — the destruction of eternal love (which wasn't what we set out to do, but rather to be the controllers of it — the same thing, since all forms of controlling or seeking to control are ultimately destructive, although, of course, not seen from that perspective by the would-be controllers).

Mercifully, the grand design protects souls in their progress towards the regaining of lost awareness from the burden of remembering most of their expressions of unawareness. In my view, it's a masochistic thing for people to try to unearth memories in order to crucify themselves — or others, which is ultimately the same thing. As you know, spiritually there's no past; consciousness only exists in the present. Even if you try to recreate a past happening in every physical detail, you cannot, because your present consciousness of it — and in it — is different; it's like a book, the reading of which gave you great pleasure at one stage and makes no impression on you years later.

In summary, what I'm saying is that forgiveness of yourself for whatever you may have unawarely done or not done is an essential ingredient in unconditional love. Once you have forgiven yourself the question of forgiving others will be irrelevant; unconditional love means accepting others as they are, so there's nothing to forgive.

Reality

10th-14th August: In your daily life there's a physical reality for which you need no proof. For example, you live in a house, you sleep in a bed, you wear clothes, you eat food, you drink liquids, you use transport of some kind, you see people, buildings, trees, fields, you are aware of your body. By and large, you take all those things for granted.

There are other kinds of reality which are commonplace to you now, for example, you press a button and you see pictures of people, places, etc., on a television screen, you turn on a radio and you hear voices, music, you go to a cinema and you see a movie in which actors are playing roles intended to present a reality which on one level you accept and on another you know is the product of the imagination of the creators of the movie and the storyline on which it is based.

You accept as reality things which are outside of your personal experience, for example, the existence of places that you have never visited, of languages that you don't know, of planets of which you have only hearsay evidence, of historical events of which you have only read or heard.

Some human beings accept other things for which they have no physical proof, such as the existence of a personal God, grace conferred through sacraments, life after death, eternal reward (Heaven), eternal punishment (Hell).

As can be seen, there are different levels of acceptance of reality in human terms, some of it unquestioning and some of it carrying uncertainty in varying degrees.

Please look now, though, at the reality that you accept without question. Everything on earth has a form or a structure and can be defined in that way. All structures are subject to change so that there is no such thing as continuity of physical form in a static state. It follows that there's no fixed reality from a human point of view. So it's hardly surprising that human beings suffer from insecurity; the human state offers no firm base, nothing which can be guaranteed to remain constant, unchanging. What is seen as reality can have no permanency about it and, in the long run, can only be an illusion.

If, then, there is a constant reality at all we have to look for it beyond the physical system. How do you create your reality? Through your feelings and thoughts. All creation originates in the mind (soul) of its creator; nothing is built in the external, physical world unless it is first designed in somebody's mind. Even what is accepted as physical reality is different for each person. If, for instance, two people look at a chair, they may agree on its colour, its type, its shape, but there are always shades of difference in the way they see it. All souls create their own individual universes — their own reality.

If one accepts that there's life after death, what continues? Not the physical body, obviously, nor any material possessions. The soul continues. What constitutes the soul? Feelings and thoughts — the reality that's created within each person. All that people take with them when their life on earth ceases is their state of being.

Each soul's reality is uniquely its own. But each soul is linked in consciousness with all other souls in God/love. The ultimate-and only-reality is in the expression of consciousness in a state of fully regained awareness. Therein lies total security.

How Best To Deal With Death

22nd - 24th August: It's a fact of life on earth that people die. Even though it hasn't happened to you yet (in this life!), you know that it will — that is, you know that your body will cease to exist. It's the vehicle that enables you to experience life on earth and when its work is done you (the soul) will leave it and it will be transformed into ashes or dust.

Nobody who has ever assumed physical form has escaped from the experience of the death and disintegration of the body. That's a categorical statement which cuts across traditional belief systems — for example, the Christian beliefs in the physical assumption into Heaven of Jesus (in his physical body) and, subsequently, in the case of some Christians, of Mary, his mother. Since Jesus was being proclaimed the only son of God, the ordinary laws of nature couldn't be seen to apply to him, nor, more arguably, to his mother. He couldn't be born in the same way as ordinary human beings, his mother couldn't go through the human process of conception, nor could they die as ordinary mortals. So myths were created and perpetuated as dogma and human beings were deprived of the very identification which Jesus wanted them to feel (with him in his humanity/divinity).

I have discussed in some detail (in our previous books) what happens to people and animals when their bodies die. Even though many people can accept that there's no death, that life on earth is simply a transitory stage in an evolutionary process designed to lead to growth in awareness, and that there's no such thing as the soul being judged and punished for its transgressions of divine law by an arbitrary God, yet physical separation is painful. No matter what one's level of awareness is, there's a deep sadness — often a desolation — about looking at the dead body of somebody one has loved, remembering the mannerisms, the way of talking, looking, touching, smiling, laughing, the association of places, a favourite chair, clothes, the grim finality of knowing that there will never again in this life-time be physical contact with that person. Even when one can feel the con-tinuity of contact in a spiritual way — and many people do and are increas-ingly allowing themselves to accept it — it's comforting, but it's just not the same as the physical presence.

In our last session we discussed the impermanence of what is seen as physical reality. It's a feature of life on earth that interpersonal relation-ships come and go. For example, two people who had a very close relation-ship with each other as school friends, went their separate ways and, on meeting many years later, find that they have little to say to each other; romantic relationships blossom, wither and die; as people move from one work situation to another, friendships with former colleagues are inevitably replaced by friendships in the new situation. The separation in many cases is just as final as physical death, although, of course, that's disguised by the fact that the people parting from each other are still in animate bodies.

People, then, are used to dealing with change and adapting themselves to it. Although many people say they don't like change, if they think about it they will see that they are managing it regularly in unconscious ways; it's such a feature of physical life that everybody has to learn to cope with it in some way; and, of course, change is designed to help growth in aware-ness.

In so far as death is concerned, it's still change, but the severity of its impact lies in the fact that it presents itself in such a final way. Accordingly, people can't adapt to it as easily as they do to other changes. (In saying that, I know that some changes, such as marriage breakdowns, can have traumatic and long-lasting effects, but there's still a possibility of physical contact, which death doesn't offer.)

How can you best deal with death? I'd like to offer the following sug-gestions:-

• don't try to be superhuman; allow yourself to grieve;

• bear in mind that each human being is really a soul with a body and that life on earth was deliberately designed for growth purposes as a tempo-rary state of being;

• don't shut yourself off from the person who has died; that soul will still want to keep in contact with you and, as long as neither of you is in a continuing depressed state, the contact will be mutually rewarding;

• when you get a feeling of contact, don't argue yourself out of it (always a logical thing to do);

• in the early stages of the separation set aside a little time each day to talk to the one who has died; don't worry if you feel a little foolish doing that — I can assure you that the soul will hear you (there's no communication more powerful than a link of love);

• send love regularly to the soul; a way of doing that was recommended in our third book (in the chapter entitled — Giving and Receiving Help; Expanding into Universal Love).

The above are some ways that I hope you will find helpful in dealing with the physical separation of death and getting on with your own life (and preparing for your own death!).

With the acceleration of growth in consciousness at present happening on earth fear of what is called the supernatural is diminishing and more people are open to the possibility of communication between souls in different dimensions. What is seen as exceptional today (or :"off the wall", depending on one's standpoint!) will become commonplace within the lifetimes of many people now on earth. As a result, separation through physical death will become much less painful than it is at present.

Mission/Purpose v Free Will

3rd September: In case of misunderstanding, I should say that my comments and suggestions in the last session are intended primarily for those who wish to preserve contact with people whose bodies have died — in other words, where there's a mutually loving bond, not a controlling one.

A question recently put to you was — "Is there a contradiction between arriving on earth with a mission/purpose and the exercise of free will?"

It is understandable that there might seem to be a contradiction but, in fact, there isn't. It is because they have free will that souls have opportunities and choices in designing broadly the purposes of their lives on earth. No soul is ever forced to live a life on earth; even a suggestion of compulsion would be an interference with free will. If a soul decides that it wants to experience a (further) life on earth it is entirely open to it to design its own purpose in as generalised or specific ways as it wishes. It has, of course, help available to it in the form of guides if it would like to avail itself of their help; that, too, is entirely a matter of choice on the part of the soul. It goes without saying that to the extent that a soul avails itself of the help of guides the greater will be the potential for growth in awareness of a life on earth.

The exercise of free will, then, is always sacrosanct. A sense of mission or purpose, which some people have very strongly, is a result of a choice freely made. How the purpose is fulfilled is also dependent on the exercise of free will. In so far as a soul's life on earth is concerned, once it takes on a body and arrives on earth the only predestined element is that the body will die. All its experiences between the birth and death of the body are governed by free will on its own part and/or on the part of others, such as, parents, teachers, religious authorities; the design of its purpose will take account of environmental conditions, usually to the extent of the conditions being deliberately chosen in order to assist the achievement of the life purpose.

Akashic Records?

12th September: From time to time you have come across the expression "akashic records" as the title given to spirit (non-material) records of the evolutionary journeys of souls on their individual paths. Are there, in fact, such records? If so, what form do they take? And how can they be explored?

In earlier times mention of records would have brought up images of mountains of paper, files, index cards, rows and rows of shelving, etc. More recently computer technology has taken over and has made access to information immeasurably easier and faster, and has also overcome physical storage problems.

We're faced with a dilemma here in terms of communication. I have repeatedly said that in spiritual terms there's no past, so how can there be a record of something that doesn't exist? Spirituality always exists in the present. You, the soul, your feelings and thoughts, your consciousness, cannot be other than in the present. You have experiences from year to year, from month to month, from week to week, from day to day, you feel and think your way through them and they help to shape your consciousness. But you cannot exist in the past. From day to day, from hour to hour, even from moment to moment, inside yourself, in your feelings and thoughts, you can only live in the present, you simply cannot relive even the experience of a second ago. So it's true to say that in spiritual (real) terms there's no past. It's also true to say that for each soul there has been a history of past experiences (the effects of which exist in its present consciousness). I think you can see that there's no contradiction between the two statements.

Given that the grand design provides for the possibility of reincarnation, it would be strange if the design didn't include facilities for each soul to study and evaluate the history of its progress towards the regaining of the awareness it had lost. So, of course, there is such a record and it is the right of each soul to have access to it. The process of getting access is much more sophisticated and more simple than anything achievable in human technological terms. It happens through an unveiling of consciousness, like a film unfolding before one's eyes.

For example, Agnes leaves her body and after a period of adjustment to her new state decides that she would like to have a look at her previous history. She doesn't have to go anywhere or to be anywhere in particular in order to fulfil her wish. She might like to have a guide with her in order to help her in assessing her progress, but that's a matter for herself. All that's needed is that she should have reached such a level of awareness that her mind is not set in any pattern of rigid beliefs, e.g., that she can accept the possibility of reincarnation, or that there's no such thing as a judgemental God. It would be easier for her if she were to ask a guide to help her. The guide would prompt her so that she would realise the extent of the information available to her; in other words, she could ask the guide to roll the film and give her a running commentary on it (in a manner of speaking!).

The information about Agnes's evolution (and every soul's) is stored in the universal consciousness, literally, in God. It's very difficult to explain that in human terms because consciousness doesn't have a tangible physical reality. It has permanence, though; so it can be said that it is eternally present, or that there's nothing but the present. Everything — every feeling, thought, action — is stored eternally in divine consciousness; nothing is ever wiped out — as happens, say, with data stored in a computer. If that seems a bit frightening, don't worry — remember that there's no judgement. It's simply that all is God and God is all infinitely and eternally and no part of God can ever not *be*.

What about the poor human trying to get information about his evolutionary history? Much progress is being made towards making information available as helpfully as possible. A lot depends on how open people are to receiving such information. If people can accept that they have guides available to help them and if they practise communicating with their guides, they will be guided to the sources of information. Usually, what will be filtered to them is whatever is relevant to their present life. People who have developed their communication are helping others to do likewise. Once conditioning is released anything is possible.

The simple answers to the questions posed at the beginning of this session is that there are permanent records of all souls' evolutionary journeys, that the records are in divine consciousness and, therefore, in each soul/oversoul, and that exploration is easier as souls grow in consciousness and can be significantly helped through communication with guides.

As an afterthought, you can see, I hope, why self-forgiveness on the part of each soul is so fundamentally essential.

Deservability

14th September: What do you deserve? Happiness? What constitutes happiness? Financial wealth? Loving relationship (s)? Good health? Physical beauty? Wide-ranging talent? Fame? Power? Inner peace? Approval by higher power (s)? Record of achievement? Fulfilling employment? Freedom of expression? Spiritual well-being? A combination of some or all of them?

One of the reasons why the evolutionary process is taking so long is that people feel that they don't deserve to be happy. How often do you find that when you're feeling happy you start wondering what's going to be round the corner to change that feeling? It's as if happiness has to be paid for by suffering of some kind, that you're not good enough to deserve it for itself.

Happiness is a feeling. Deservability is controlled by thought which is conditioned by subconscious influences and imposes itself on feeling. From the moment of birth people are classified as sinners, unworthy recipients of God's love. Even if they're not born into a religious environment, they are still more likely than not to be subject to more criticism than praise.

It's not possible for a person to be happy on a continuing basis without thinking that he deserves to be happy; otherwise he'll think himself out of feeling happy. Rather than let his pattern of thinking impose itself on his feelings, which is the way conditioning works, he needs to allow his feelings to expand his thought processes. Ultimately, happiness on a continuing basis can be a reality only when a soul feels at one with God/love, with the result that feelings and thoughts are completely in balance and there is no conditioned influence.

Everybody deserves to be happy. There can be no doubt about that because every soul is a part of God. It is understandable that souls are imbued with a sense of unworthiness since they deliberately separated themselves from their real selves, i.e., God/love in them. Once they allow their own divinity the question of deservability no longer arises.

No matter where we travel with our sessions we keep coming back to unconditional love. There's no other way.

Sexual Energy in "The New Consciousness"

19th-21st September: Let's have a look at a question asked at a recent meeting — "Can you redefine sexual energy and its present force in the new consciousness?"

It goes without saying that sex has been a potent force in the history of human evolution. (I'm using the word 'sex' here in terms of interaction between people rather than literally as gender.) People enjoy it, become obsessed with it, abuse others through it, use it as a power base, run away from it, see it as a duty, sell it, sacrifice it to their God, consider themselves deprived if it doesn't figure in their lives — and sometimes if it does! One way or another it impinges on people's lives in significant ways.

I need to make a distinction here between sexual energy and what is known as sexual intercourse. It would be a basic mistake to think of sex exclusively in terms of a sexual act between two people. Its most obvious expression is as the source of procreation which has tended to create confusion in people's minds to the extent of either seeing its sole purpose in that light, or as a potentially pleasurable activity which incidentally has a procreative capacity. But many people, either through choice or through circumstances outside of their control, don't experience direct sexual interaction in the form of sexual intercourse. That doesn't mean, though, that their sexual energy is necessarily suppressed; it is, only, if they allow themselves to become obsessed about the lack of such experience.

Fundamentally, sexual energy is about creativity. In the final analysis, what really affects people most and limits them is a lack of creative expression in their lives. Life on earth is structured in such a way that people need money (or its equivalent) to survive. In order to obtain money people have to find remunerative employment or become dependent on social assistance of some kind — unless they're amongst the favoured few who have substantial private incomes. In many cases (most likely, the vast majority) the work that people do in order to provide income for themselves and their families, where relevant, is, from their perspective, repetitive and unfulfilling; unfortunately, it's the exception rather than the rule for people to find their work both spiritually and financially rewarding.

In consideration of this question the increasing impact of technology is significant. Amongst other things, technology is designed to take care of boring, routine tasks, and it does. It is, consequently, expected to leave people with time for more productive work. It certainly means that people have more time on their hands, but the challenge of finding income-producing work is often daunting, if not insuperable, Resulting worry then suppresses creativity.

An ideal would be utopian societies, nation/states, where all people would have available to them soul-satisfying outlets of expression without having to be concerned about survival in financial terms. That situation is not likely to be generally attainable for many years yet; but the more people can achieve it in individual ways, the sooner it will be.

To answer the question, I would redefine sexual energy as creativity. All people are creative; it's impossible for a part of God not to be creative. Sexual energy, then, is inseparably linked with the overall creativity of being, and that energy is present in everybody without exception. It can find outlets through all forms of creative expression, by which I mean generally how people approach whatever they do, whether it be writing a book or a poem or a play, or painting a picture, or taking a photograph, or sculpting, or embroidery, or flower-arranging, or gardening, or designing a building, or cooking, or computer programming, or healing in its many forms, or farming, or film-making, or acting, or sports, or travelling, or resting, or whatever form of activity presents itself for them. What I'm saying really is that all human activity has to be creative because all human beings are creative. Once they accept that, their self-esteem is raised, the flow of their energy is released and opportunities for more and more self-expression become available to them.

Ask yourself — suppose you were in a situation where you'd never have to bother about earning money, what would you want to do with your life? Having answered the question, project the answer into your present income-needing situation.

For example, Paula is employed in a secretarial position which has long since ceased to offer her any challenge; that in itself, of course, is a tribute to her capacity in applying her organisational flair to the job. One day she decides to have a look at what she would really like to do; the answer she comes up with is that she'd love to be a journalist.

Apart from the fact that she can't afford to leave her job, she would have to go through a long process of training and there would be no guarantee that she would be acceptable as a candidate, let alone that she'd find an opportunity, for employment. Is, then, this exercise of looking into what she'd want a waste of time? Paula has used her creative energy in her approach to her secretarial job. Now she needs to bring that energy into fulfilling her dream. Her job provides her with a cushion to help her on her way, perhaps to do a course in journalism, or creative writing, or to join a creative writing group. In her life experience, including her work, she may well find interesting material which she may be able to use as a basis for an article or a feature. Because she has her job so well organised she may have some spare time during the day which she could devote to, say, research into a somewhat esoteric subject which might yet be of interest to many people. She has freedom to experiment because she's not dependent for survival on getting an income through journalism, so she can send her articles out to newspapers, magazines, etc.

If, as would be likely to happen, she only gets rejection slips (or ignored) initially, she'll have the honour of sharing the early experience of most successful writers. Even if she never becomes a full-time journalist, she will have opened up for herself a vast outlet of creative expression and, in the process, brought a lot of enjoyment into her life, with the result that, incidentally, her secretarial job is now much more satisfying. Thus, her creative energy is no longer suppressed and she is more fully expressing herself, including her sexuality.

If I may move from the particular to the general, then, what I'm suggesting is that people don't dismiss their dreams, their fantasies, that what may seem to be impossible may be achievable in indirect ways and that their very situation (job, etc.), which may seem to be totally restrictive, may, in fact, help them on their way. Seeing things from a different perspective will free their energy, of which, of course, their sexuality is an integral part.

Money

26th September-2nd October: I think that nobody will dispute that money occupies a central place in most people's thoughts. People have to find money every day for basic necessities — food, shelter, etc. Some people (a minority) don't have to concern themselves about money in the sense of not having enough to meet day to day needs; but they are likely to be involved in financial activities, such as speculating on the stock market, studying investment possibilities, considering business opportunities, funding payrolls, buying and selling in some form. No matter what people do, whether it's going to a supermarket, or a shop, or a public house, or a hairdresser, or a cinema, or a football match, or indeed almost anywhere one can imagine, unless it's just for a walk, they need money. People worry themselves sick over money, burden themselves with heavy debts, rob each other, sometimes even kill each other, for money, they play lotteries, they fantasise about winning big amounts of money, those who can get paid employment spend a major part of their lives working, often in unsatisfying jobs, for meagre, yet necessary, incomes. People can't even die respectably without leaving money behind them for the disposal of their bodily remains. And I need hardly comment on how much energy is centred on wills (or the lack of them).

One of the biggest problem areas where money is concerned is in what tends to be seen as a conflict between the spiritual and physical or material worlds. I'm assuming that people who don't believe in life beyond what they experience on earth don't have any difficulties around the concept of money — the concept, as distinct from the actuality of whether they have enough money for their needs or fantasies. Accordingly, I'm addressing myself to those who believe that people are a continuity of spirit, that when they are finished with their bodies they move on to another dimension of existence.

As you know, it's part of the culture that has evolved through the ages around the expression of spirituality that that expression involves rejection of the physical or material. But, if people are spiritual beings, souls with bodies rather than bodies with souls, if they accept that they continue to exist as souls, why are they on earth at all? Surely it must be in order to experience whatever earth has to offer so that they can learn from that experience and grow in awareness or consciousness? And, since money plays such a central role in the earth experience, they as souls must have something valuable to learn from how to deal with it. In my view, if people go through life without learning how to deal with money they will have missed out on an important opportunity for growth in (spiritual) awareness.

I know I'm repeating myself in saying that the purpose of life on earth for people is, fundamentally and essentially, to free themselves from a feeling of separation into a feeling of unity or oneness. At the root of their feeling of separation is their concept of God. If they put God into a mould separate from themselves they are placing a limit on themselves (as well as, of course, on God) and, in that limitation, they are separating themselves from themselves. But if, and once, they can accept that all life (everything, the lot, including themselves) is contained in God, they know that there's no separation between the worlds of spirit and earth, that all is spirit, that earth operates as an aid to the spiritual, that the energy of God/love infuses all creation — and creation inevitably, ineluctably, includes money as things are at present organised on earth.

It is clear, then, — at least in my view — that people as individuals actually own nothing on earth. (Contained in God they own everything.) They have a loan of things — their bodies, whatever they use, including, of course, money. All the things of earth are part of a flowing cycle of energy, going in, out, round and round. Money is an expression of energy. People need it to survive on earth like they need air or water, but, just as they don't own air or water, they don't own money. If they become obsessive about owning money — as, indeed, about any form of ownership (including possessiveness of spouses, lovers, children) — they block the flow of energy and place severe limitations on their growth in consciousness. When they accept and feel themselves in union with God they have freedom to give and receive, to let all the energy of the universe work through them, for them, in them , helping themselves and all others. Their guides, of course, help them towards that union and, in the process, to expand more and more into their higher selves or oversouls.

If you don't own any money how can you pay your bills? You don't own your bills either, although you often tend to act as if you do; you curse them, worry about them, resist them. I suggest that you try to let go of all resistance to them and to see them as part of the flow of energy. It may take a while (a few weeks!) for you to reach the stage of giving whoops of delight when bills find you. But it will get easier. I suggest that you remind yourself that paying your bills is a form of giving; and, in not resisting giving, it will be easier for you not to resist receiving, either; bear in mind that it's all expression of divine energy and that you're privileged — and entitled — to share in that expression. Knowing that the flow of divine energy never falters — can never falter — you can let yourself trust in the infinite supply of that energy — and even say "thanks" for the opportunity to pay yet another bill!

Auras, Etc.

30th September - 5th October: In our earlier session on the subject of control I intimated that the most effective way, in my opinion, of keeping one's aura clear is to ask one's guides to do so. How, then, is it that, for example, somebody who works as a therapist and who, although she asked her guides to keep her aura clear, was still very much affected by clients, even to the extent of experiencing some of their physical symptoms?

The aura, sometimes called the etheric body, is the spirit counterpart of the physical body. It is a body of light and can be seen as such. It follows the shape of the physical body and when people die they are recognisably similar in their etheric bodies to their appearances in their physical bodies. The aura is really the person in spirit form on earth so that, in fact, people are present on earth in both physical and spirit forms. When the physical body dies the aura leaves it and continues to evolve on its journey in spirit.

In case of misunderstanding, I must emphasise that the aura is not the soul; as I have explained earlier, soul is synonymous with mind, through feelings, thoughts, consciousness. The soul can only be seen through taking on form, such as physical, etheric bodies, etc.

People sometimes get lost in complex distinctions between etheric, astral, causal, etc., bodies. That's a way of putting form on levels of awareness or consciousness. It is analogous to, say, hierarchical systems where people, as they move up the ladder, get to wear different clothes. While there are no hierarchical systems in spirit, souls are distinguishable according to their levels of awareness.

The aura foreshadows and reflects the condition of the physical body. Even though the aura, since it is not physical, cannot suffer damage through, say, illness or accidents, it can be affected by such happenings. That's why, for instance, if a person dies in a debilitated condition after a long illness, the etheric body needs a period of recuperation. It's all linked in with the soul, of course; both the physical and etheric bodies are vehicles for the soul. Both are affected by the soul's state of consciousness.

When I talk about keeping the aura clear, then, what do I mean? And how can guides do that? Guides don't (can't) interfere with free will. If you decide to run across a busy road without looking to either side of you, you may get knocked down (or cause somebody else to get knocked down!). If you neglect your body's needs, it may get ill. If you drink too much alcohol, you may wake up in the company of a hangover. If you take on burdens of guilt, worry, etc., you may feel tired and stressed.

If you ask your guides to keep your aura clear, it gives them freedom (a) to make sure that no spirit being can attempt to control you in any way, and (b) to help you, without interfering with your free will, avoid damage through physical interaction, including controlling thoughts directed at you by a human being.

Let's go back to the case of the therapist mentioned in the first paragraph above. On her request to them to keep her aura clear her guides would automatically have placed what I can only describe as an energy shield around her aura. The nearest analogy I can give you in physical terms is an electric fence. Suppose a mischievous soul decided to invade her aura it would receive such a shock that it would immediately conclude, in a manner of speaking, that she was too hot to handle; in fact, all souls coming near her would know automatically that her aura was impenetrable. That doesn't mean, though, that souls in spirit can't communicate with her; they can, but the communication is overseen by her guides who act as filters, rather like secretaries who are continuously on duty and who make sure that she is constantly minded.

While she is still human she is interacting with other humans on a daily basis. This is in line with her life purpose and, of course, she is affected in one way or another by the people she meets. That's her choice on her evolutionary journey. Keeping her aura clear won't stop her getting tired, or feeling pain, or becoming ill, or won't prevent her body ageing and eventually dying; these are the incidental challenges of living on earth. When she is tired she needs rest, when she is ill she needs healing, when the burden of years lies heavy on her she needs to be philosophical. If she is doing something, or going into a situation, which is likely to be physically damaging for her, her guides will put opportunities in her way to avert the damage. She may not respond initially to the subtle signals designed to divert her from the situation; if she doesn't, ways of repairing the damage will present themselves to her. Since she has been so aware as to align herself with the evolved energy of the universe — which is the effect of asking her guides to keep her aura clear — she need never fear that she will be neglected, even for an instant.

Beings From Other Planets?

12th October: Question: "Do beings from other planets inspire and direct us? Are they helping us move to the next dimension?"

You may remember that in our first book I used an example of a soul choosing, for growth purposes, to experience temporary evolution on the planet Uranus. As I stated then, earth is the only planet on which there is, at present, materialisation, as you know it, although spirit life can simulate the conditions of earth without its density of form.

It is very difficult for you to conceive of life existing outside of place (or time). Even though you have never physically experienced life on other planets you can accept that they exist because they have been absorbed into the structure of human comprehension. So it is easier for you to picture existence, whatever its form, centred in a place, albeit an unfamiliar one, such as another planet, rather than existence in no place. It would follow then, I think, that guidance coming from (spirit) beings on other planets might have a more readily comprehensible ring to it than guidance coming from spirit beings who don't seem to have any base (a place to call home!).

All creation, including all planets, exists for the use of souls, who are always free to choose how they express themselves; in other words, at different stages they may choose to experience repeated lives on earth or a combination of lives on earth as well as on another or other planets. That means that some souls who are now on earth in physical bodies have also experienced life on other planets (in non-physical bodies). There are many "aliens" now living on earth! There's nothing sinister about that, by the way; souls are souls, no matter what form their expression takes. (Incidentally, that explains why some souls find difficulty in "earthing" themselves; they're not familiar with the ways of the planet.)

The grand design envisages that human beings are helped by guides specially assigned to them through their own choice. There are also guides, spirit beings, angels, archangels, whatever you like to call them, who are overseeing the operation of the planet generally, not in a controlling way, but always seeking to provide opportunities for growth in consciousness. As we have seen in other sessions, souls in spirit are constantly in communication with human beings; people's awareness of that depends on their openness and capacity to receive the communications. So of course, souls who happen to be on other planets communicate with, or try to communicate with, human beings. How inspirational the communications are depends on the levels of awareness of the communicators, as also does whether they attempt to direct, if that word is being used as meaning 'control' rather than 'guide'.

At present, most souls now on earth have not chosen to have guides specifically assigned to them. Accordingly, they are more open to indiscriminate communication from spirit sources, including those on other planets, than those who have so chosen. As you know, guidance is usually arranged before a soul takes on a physical body, but if at any time during a physical lifetime a person decides to ask for a guide or guides there are billions of evolved souls who would love such assignments. When one soul is helped all souls are helped through the interlinking of consciousness.

Imagination

19th October - 21st November: We have been discussing reality, creativity, how souls express themselves. I want to include imagination in our consideration since it keeps cropping up as, at least, a question mark in the area of communication with guides.

If you look for alternative meanings for imagination you'll find words such as fancy, creativity, insight, inspiration, sensitivity, vision, inventiveness. In an earlier session (in our second book) I described imagination as the language of the soul; creativity, insight, inspiration, also seem suitable.

People often portray themselves, or are portrayed, as having no imagination. For them, presumably, imagination would be seen to belong exclusively to those involved in obviously creative expression, such as, poets, novelists, script writers, painters, sculptors, inventors, entrepreneurs. But, of course, that's not the case; a soul cannot *be* without imagination.

Each soul creates its own universe; no two souls see anything in exactly the same way. Your imagination is ceaselessly active. If somebody mentions a bird to you , you immediately imagine a bird; similarly with a flower, or a tree, or a ship, or an aeroplane, no matter what it is, an image of some kind will form in your mind. When you're reading, you're constantly imagining what you're reading. What might be regarded as the most functional of work cannot be done without imagination. For example, a carpenter cannot make a table without imagining it first; neither can a farmer plant a row of potatoes, nor a cleaner clean a window.

Ironically, even though it's true that many people see themselves as having little or no imagination, it is often the same people who will dismiss as "just my imagination" insights, thoughts, that come to them "out of the blue"; in the process, they are, at least, acknowledging that they have imagination.

A central difficulty in so far as imagination is concerned is that it tends to be controlled by limitations of what is known. For example, if somebody asks you to imagine a bird, you will create a picture in your mind of a bird that you have seen; or, if somebody mentions an orange or an apple to you, you will picture them as you remember having seen them. Suppose I ask you to imagine being happy, what happens? Or, if you're feeling happy, can you imagine being unhappy? Let's take the questioning a step further. You accept that souls will ultimately regain full awareness and will then have reached a state of total happiness and fulfilment — a heavenly state of complete unity with God/love. Try to imagine how that state might be. The best you can do with it will probably be to equate heaven with your image of complete happiness; and, of course, what happiness means to you is constantly changing as your awareness changes. And that's the way it is. Heaven is a state of being which is constantly evolving even in the ultimate state of full awareness.

Heaven is, of course, automatically linked with God. We have discussed God at some length in other sessions and arrived at a description of God as love or feeling and all its expressions. How can you imagine God, though? You don't have to go looking for an image of God. Wherever you are, God is. In every person you meet, God is. In all life, God is. God expresses for you in all your creativity. In whatever you imagine, God is. So, you see, you don't have to involve yourself in strenuous efforts to create an image of God; all you need do is look around you wherever you are and whom ever or whatever you see or feel or hear or touch or perceive in any way you are in the presence of God, within you and without you. In that way your imagination and reality are inseparably linked; in fact, they are one and the same thing.

You may remember that in an earlier session I indicated that every feeling, thought, action is stored in divine consciousness; imaginings are, of course, included.

In the non-physical (spirit) state it's easier to understand the reality of imagination. In the spirit state creation is instantaneous; all a soul in spirit has to do is to imagine something and it is. It's like, say, having a magic lantern, wishing for something and there it is in front of you. The form will not be material, of course, so whatever you have imagined can be caused to disappear as simply as it has manifested. When a soul is free in itself you can imagine (!) how enjoyable the spirit state is; as you know, life on earth is intended to help it attain freedom.

Part II

What is Life on Planet Earth Going to be Like in the Future?

I

9th December 1994 - 15th January 1995: Now that we're at the end of one year and the beginning of another in your time framework you would like me to outline in some detail how I see the future of planet earth. I hasten to say that what I'm giving here is my vision of how the planet will ideally evolve, and I'm stressing that it's my vision and not an immutable pattern of evolution. As you know, the existence of free will makes it impossible to say in a black and white way that this is how it's all going to be. Nonetheless, my vision is in line with the aims of the grand design and the trend of its implementation..

It is quite clear, I think, that the pace of evolution has accelerated to a remarkable degree in this century. This has reflected itself very obviously in the technological revolution that has taken place. What has been happening in the field of technology is part of an overall changing consciousness which has been exciting for many people, disturbing for many others, and both exciting and disturbing for still many others. Institutional arrangements, which had seemed to be unbreakable in their solidity, have been rocked to their foundations, leadership has had to find new expression, people are no longer prepared to accept that their lives can be controlled within rigid frameworks of rules and regulations, the emphasis on finding individual freedom of expression has radically increased. Inevitably, of course, there's a backlash. What has come to be called fundamentalism is stretching out its tentacles to clutch within its grasping arms those who are still looking for security in being told — this you must do — or — this you must not do — and then you will forever be rewarded or punished depending on how you behave yourself —.

Understandably, given all the changes that have been taking place, this has been a century of many contrasts. There have been wars on a scale that the world has never before experienced. People have behaved, and are still behaving, towards each other with cruelty of such proportions that it is almost inconceivable how free will could, and can, be exercised in such horrific ways. On the other hand, many barriers of rigid class distinctions (which were the source of widespread, but seemingly socially respectable and acceptable, forms of cruelty for many centuries) have been broken down. Governmental systems have apparently become increasingly democratic, admittedly not without much struggle, and bloodshed, in many cases. Most significantly, the level and the extent of world-wide communication processes have increased so dramatically that news of what's happening almost anywhere in the world is now more or less instantly available. Injustices, barbarities, atrocities, man's inhumanity to man, are now highlighted to such an extent that nobody, no matter how secure his position seems to be, can any longer be sure of escaping detection if he is a participant in such activities.

What tends to be considered newsworthy, of course, is still, generally, negatively focused. What are regarded as scandalous happenings create more sensational headlines than recording the achievements of so many who are unobtrusively working to help people find peace and fulfilment in their lives. Accordingly, it would be superficially reasonable for somebody who regularly reads newspapers and/or looks and listens to television and/or listens to radio to conclude that the state of the world is getting worse rather than better. Yet, in my view, there is no doubt but that planet earth is now an infinitely better place in which to live than it has ever been. Platforms are now being provided for people who are at present experiencing life on earth, and for those being born and to be born into physical bodies, to create states of being which could literally be described as heaven on earth. What sort of states would/will those be?

Once again, I think it would be helpful to attempt to answer that question by way of an illustration.

II

Because of the breakthrough in consciousness that has been taking place in recent times and is continuing to happen, the key to which is acceptance of divinity in humanity, in other words, no separation from God/love, it is now possible to envisage a state within the physical system which would serve as a model for the further evolution of earth in the fulfilment of its purpose of helping souls to regain lost awareness. This would not be a re-creation of the Atlantean model, although it would have fundamentally the same motivation.

In the context of the illustration it is appropriate not to pinpoint an existing identifiable location. The word 'utopia' has been incorporated into everyday language and is taken to mean an ideal condition or situation. So it would suit, I think, to call our model state utopia.

I'm going to use the present tense in describing utopia even though I'm giving it a birth date thirty years into the future. I'm doing this in the interests of simplicity and easy reading as well as to give the new state an immediacy of existence.

Utopia is a small country with a population of about four million people. It is not a new country, but it was divided under different governmental jurisdictions until 2025 when it was reunited into one state. It is entirely independent in its administration of its own affairs.

It so happened, and, of course, this was no accident, that the people who inhabit the new state were at the forefront of the emerging consciousness of the twentieth century. As I mentioned in an earlier session, souls tend to reincarnate in groups, sometimes quite large groups. It was part of the purpose of the souls who were born into that location, or who moved into it from other areas, during the later twentieth and early twenty first centuries, that they should create a way of being in the physical dimension which would mirror as far as possible life in spirit at the fourth stage of evolutionary growth and which, ideally, might be an inspiration to others, and that thus all the inequalities, injustices, deprivation and pain, which still, unfortunately, are inherent in the human experience, would more quickly be eradicated, so that the planet would no longer be a vale of tears but a joyful interlude in unfolding consciousness.

Initially, when the new utopian state came into being, it inherited a governmental system which followed broadly the outline of twentieth century democracies. For example, it had a president and a parliament, all elected for specific terms by the votes of the people. The membership of the parliament consisted of representatives of different political groupings, who presented themselves and their policies to the people; the numerical parliamentary strength of each party was dependent on its popularity with the electorate. The aim of each party was to have an overall majority so that it could form a government on its own. If, after an election, no party emerged with such a majority, the alternatives were to form a coalition of two or more parties or to hold another election.

The president was also elected by popular vote and was the first citizen, with prescribed constitutional powers.

There were institutions of state which were outside of the political system but subject to political heads who formed the membership of the government. These included the civil service and security arrangements, e.g., policing, military and custodial. Courts of law were independent bodies in the execution of their jurisdiction, although not in so far as the appointment of the judiciary was concerned; in practice, the government exercised that function.

In theory, all power vested in the people. In practice, this was so in so far as the people by their votes decided who should exercise that power on their behalf.

In earlier times the spread of population was rurally oriented, but as the twentieth century progressed people moved to cities in large numbers. Major adjustments were required in the provision of amenities, such as, housing, transport, medical facilities, water, sewerage, electricity, heating, telecommunications, employment, welfare. The shift towards urbanisation marked a radical departure from a society, where generally everybody within a community knew everybody else, to a more anonymous way of life, which suited some people and didn't suit others.

Religions were mainly Christian in denomination with small minority groupings, such as, Jewish, Buddhist. The Christian religions were mainly Roman Catholic, Anglican, Presbyterian, Methodist. Traditionally, there were many tensions between the Roman Catholic and the other Christian religions. The hierarchical authoritarianism of the Roman Catholic religion and the biblical fundamentalism of some of the other religions were severely tested and dented as the twentieth century drew to a close.

While the democratic system did not, in theory, allow for class distinctions, there were many inequalities; for example, large numbers of people could not find remunerative employment and had to survive on meagre welfare allowances, pyramidal hierarchical structures were the order of the day, with, inevitably, the vast majority of workers serving at the bases of the pyramids and finding little fulfilment in their work, many people, particularly older people, lived in isolated penury. The poverty of external circumstances often tended to create spiritual aridity which was not helped by too facile answers to the effect that suffering was the way to find happiness in a heaven which was impossible to conceptualise.

III

In our first book I outlined different stages in a soul's journeying to a state of full, or, more accurately, fully-regained awareness. For the sake of clarity and simplicity I divided the process into seven stages, with the seventh being the ultimate one. The first and second stages combine a mixture of continuity of life in physical and non-physical bodies. Souls who have reached the fourth stage (to which I have referred earlier in this chapter) still, if they wish, incarnate/reincarnate in physical bodies; they do so with the object of helping others to grow in consciousness.

What's happening in the present shift in consciousness is that the spiritual and physical worlds are being moved closer together. It's much easier now than it would have been even as recently as twenty years ago to envisage a time when the barriers between the worlds will be broken down completely, as they are partially at present, and continuing communication will be possible (although maybe not always desired!) between souls still in physical bodies and those who have left the physical scene (at least temporarily).

In describing the fourth stage (in our first book) I concentrated mainly on the guidance aspect of it — in other words, how souls at that stage acted as guides to human beings. What I'd like to do now is to take the process further by describing in some detail how life functions at the fourth stage — in its spirit manifestation — and then to endeavour to represent how all that transfers to our utopian state. Utopia couldn't work in physical terms if the people inhabiting it hadn't reached the level of awareness of the fourth stage.

IV

First things first. Souls at the fourth stage fully accept their own divinity; they are in God, God is in them, there's no separation. They don't have any physical problems, such as, illness, tiredness, ageing, disability, the need for food, clothing, shelter, money. Obviously all that makes a big difference! In a real sense,there's no government, no religion, there are no bureaucratic institutions, no laws, no rules or regulations, — or no traffic jams!

In talking about souls at the fourth stage I'm really referring to what I have described elsewhere as oversouls — in other words, souls expressing their fullness of being, of consciousness. They have ready access to all knowledge, so that, of course, there's no need — I stress the word need — for schools or colleges or universities as vehicles of learning. Memory, as you know it within the physical system, is no longer necessary. Souls are identifiable in their individuality and appearance. Of course, they don't have material bodies but they appear to each other in forms which are expressive of the essence of each soul in its uniqueness.

In order to attempt to make life at the fourth stage comprehensible to you I'll have to use an approach of comparison with what you know.

The range of people's activities on earth is multi-aspected. The following are some examples — in no presumed order of preference — of how people find satisfaction and enjoyment and fulfilment:- reading, writing, painting, photography, film-making, film-viewing, gardening, walking, swimming, athletics, cooking, travel, holidays, sleeping, eating, drinking, television, radio, nature, driving, flying, making money, winning prizes, toys, farming, successful business deals, achieving recognition in their careers, loving relationship with children/adults/animals, solitude, being at peace with themselves and the world around them, causes, charities, material comforts, shopping, home-making, giving and receiving gifts, special occasions, football matches, concerts, birthdays, weddings, ideas, discussion, listening to music, politics, horse/motor/cycle racing, playing golf, cards; crosswords, computers, technology generally, wood carving, sculpture, pottery, tapestry, relaxing, massage, therapeutic activities generally, design , invention, scholarship, skilled workmanship, acting, appearance, making clothes, jewellery, religious practices, meditation, making love, intimacy, communicating with their guides/guardian angels, feeling at one with God/love.

There are many others that I deliberately didn't include, such as, gambling, drug-taking, alcoholism, quarrelling, physical fighting, accumulating possessions, robbery, gossiping, pornography, abuse, domination, manipulation, cheating, hunting, one-upmanship, bigotry, dogmatism, sexual promiscuity, exclusivity, prostitution, violence generally. While aspects of some of these may be present in my earlier list of examples, it is doubtful, I suggest, that they could be seen as meeting all three categories of satisfaction, enjoyment and fulfilment; temporarily, maybe, but not indefinitely.

It would be strange indeed if life in spirit were to be so totally different from life on earth that forms of expression which occasion enjoyment on earth would no longer be possible in spirit. (When I use the expression 'in spirit' in this chapter I mean the fourth stage.) A logical expectation, I assume, would be that people would find much more expanded possibilities of fulfilment within the areas that interest them. The question is — how?

In order to answer the question as clearly as I can I propose to concentrate on certain areas which are of broad general relevance to human beings. I'm using 'you' in a general way.

Artistic expression: Suppose you are interested in reading novels where a large contributory factor to your enjoyment is in the unfolding of the stories. If you knew how the story was going to end before you started reading a book a lot of the pleasure of the experience would be taken from you. (In fact, you would probably be annoyed if somebody told you the outcome of the story before you had a chance to read it.) The same thing is true of looking at a movie, or listening to, say, a radio play or being a spectator at a sporting event, or, indeed, anything where the evolving experience is filled with expectancy. If, in spirit, there's no beginning and no ending, and you know it all anyway, how can you get the same, not to mention more, enjoyment from reading, looking at movies, etc.?

The simple answer is that in spirit everything is the way you want it to be. As you know, even within the space of one lifetime on earth, your tastes in what brings you enjoyment, e.g., literature, are continually evolving. That's also true in spirit. If you want to read a novel and you don't want to know how it ends, you can have that experience. You have unlimited ability to create whatever you wish, including temporary suspension of your awareness/insight/ knowledge. It is unimaginable that somebody who enjoys, say, words, languages, the look and the feeling of books, would be deprived of that pleasure. There's no problem with words or with languages in spirit. Even though, as I have explained in an earlier session, they are not necessary for communication, since that's achieved in more complete ways without them, yet they are available — of course, since everything is — in whatever form you wish. You can have a most wonderful library, with beautifully bound books, if you so desire. If you have written books while on earth, you can have them on your shelves, if you like. Needless to say, the books and the bookshelves are not material, but they are real — and real in a permanent way, if that's what you want, not in a temporary state as on earth.

I imagine you can easily understand that what applies to books equally applies to, say, movies or television or radio or painting or writing or sculpting or pottery or wood carving or carpentry or music or choreography or flower arranging or design or gardening or cooking or sports or any and every artistic expression, including vehicles for such expression, e.g., theatres, cinemas, wood. You can approach any of them at whatever level you like.

Sexual expression: I've put this into a separate category because it occupies such a significant place in human existence.

As you know, the division of the human race into male and female genders was incorporated into the grand design not alone for procreative purposes but also as an aid to growth in consciousness. The possibility of reincarnation allows for a variety of experience through male and female lives on earth.

When souls reach the fourth stage the sexual distinction between male and female is no longer needed. But what if you wish to retain it? Then, of course, that's possible. Sexual expression is, ideally, about achieving unity, a depth of intimate communication. In our opening session in this book I talked about special relationships. The most exquisite, ecstatic union is achievable in spirit. In your human state you can have loving relationships with many people but you continually search for a soul mate as the ultimate in sexual intimacy. Needless to say, in spirit there is complete unity of communication in the most intimate possible ways with your soul mate. There's no such institution as marriage in spirit. There's no need for the rules of conduct that human societies seem to find necessary to establish.

Religious expression: For many people religious expression is a way of life. The human evolution has given birth to a great variety of religions. I need hardly dwell on how much energy has gone into religious devotion, with all its rituals, dogmas, rules, institutions, hierarchies, provision of places of worship, security, altruism, bigotry, intolerance, cruelty, division, solicitude — so much conflicting manifestation. The central difficulty about religions — and it is a fundamental, inescapable, difficulty — is that they haven't come to terms with God. They teach that God is omnipotent, omniscient, omnipresent, that 'man is created in the image of God' — but the meaning of all that seems to elude them. In any case, as I have repeatedly said, God does not exist in terms of a Supreme Being but is rather the divinity in all souls and in all creativity and all creation endlessly evolving, incapable of definition or limitation. Souls in spirit are fully aware of this, and that awareness is part of their being, so that they are at one with God. That's the ever constant search for humans of course, — the search for the lost God in them — or, more accurately, the imprisoned God.

Well, you are now familiar with the pattern. Souls in spirit can have all the religious expression they want with whatever attendant rituals they would like to have. Needless to say, they know (at the fourth stage, I repeat, in case of confusion) that it's all a game.

Political expression: Physical restrictions have developed a perception of the desirability of ordered societies on earth. For example, people's needs for money, shelter, food, transport, roads, schools, hospitals, shops, had to be met. Increased urbanisation has involved the introduction of systems for the ordered flow of traffic through say, queuing, traffic lights. There are always people who, for varying reasons, want to be regulators. Thus what has come to be known as politics evolved with all its institutional frameworks.

The same needs don't exist in spirit. So monarchs, presidents, governments, civil service, courts, security arrangements, all the incidental trappings with which you are familiar, are not alone unnecessary but, in so far as they are sources of elitism, would imply class distinction or orders of precedence which have no place (in a manner of speaking!) in spirit.

As you know, some people love politics, whether as active participants or backstage debaters. How could they possibly enjoy themselves in spirit if there was no scope for political expression?

Here again, all things are possible. An analogy would be helpful, I think. You know how children love to invent games. They play the games with great intensity and seriousness — and enjoyment — but they also know, although they have suspended that knowledge, that they are playing games. Adults in the physical world have lost so much of what they had as children. People are born as children to give them fresh opportunities, yes, but also because they carry with them familiarity with the world of spirit while being temporarily free from the clutter of conditioning.

So, while there are no children in spirit (please bear in mind that I'm using the expression 'in spirit' to describe the fourth stage) souls can, if they wish, become as children and play whatever games they like with, believe me, deep levels of passion, but they know they are playing games; they, too, have just suspended that knowledge while they are involved in the games.

Sporting Expression: I mentioned sports in the artistic section but I'm giving them a special category of their own because they occupy such a central place in the lives of many people that they would be loath even to try to imagine any state of being that would not allow them to continue that interest. For those who wish to participate in sporting activities, the hard work, such as training, can be eliminated and they can just get on with playing the games. There's no difficulty about getting teams together, who can create their own rules — and limitations — for the duration of the games. Again, of course, they all know that they're only playing games, but that doesn't interfere with the spirit of the play (if you'll excuse the pun!). You can participate in leagues and/or cups and/or tournaments to your soul's (!) desire. You can also, of course, enjoy being a spectator, if you so wish.

Spiritual expression: I only include this as a category in the interest of clarity. All expression is, of course, spiritual. As I have already said, souls in spirit fully accept themselves and their own divinity, so there's never any separation from God, no matter what games they play. Accordingly, there can be no intolerance, no judgementalism, no attempts to control or dominate, just unconditional love in practice.

V

I should mention here that while the physical system is a vehicle for growth in awareness it is also intended to be, in its evolution, a paradise or a divine playground. That will only be achieved if and when the fourth stage can be brought fully into human manifestation. I have chosen to use an example of an imaginary utopian state for illustration purposes, but that's not intended to promote elitism, or the idea of a specially chosen race; obviously, what we're really talking about is a state of consciousness, of being, which is independent of location and not limited in any way. At the same time, there's a gradualism in the way things evolve in the physical world; so it is well to pinpoint some location and start from there.

Now for the big question — how can the spirit and human states merge in our utopia?

VI

The primary ingredient is awareness, or consciousness. As I have already said, the people who inhabit utopia in the year 2025 are fully aware of themselves and accept themselves and their own divinity within their humanness. They have come together in accordance with arrangements made before they reincarnated. Their aim is to bring the fourth stage into human existence.

Since they are now in physical bodies they are subject to the restrictiveness that that involves. Accordingly, there will still have to be arrangements by which people can cooperate with each other in creating opportunities for all to live satisfying, fulfilling and enjoyable lives. A comprehensive process of reform is set in motion once the new state is born.

A fundamental premise of the new setup is that there are, and will be, no hierarchies, no discrimination, no deprivation. It is a truism that power corrupts, and hierarchical systems inevitably lead to abuse of power. This was basically the reason for the original fall from awareness, the separation from God, which must never be allowed to happen again (without interfering with free will, of course).

Work features, naturally, but it is seen as creative expression, not as labour. All the people in the state, without exception, are provided with opportunities to experience fulfilling employment — or no employment, if that's their wish. However, it's the nature of soul to have areas of interest, so that it will always find outlets for its creativity once it has the freedom to do so.

But, you ask, how can some form of hierarchical establishment be avoided since in order to initiate reforms, or, indeed, to make anything happen at all, there have to be leaders — or at least, one leader?

To enable the new state to come into being some people had to take initiatives. Those people were some of the participants in the governments of the previously fragmented state. Because they had reached an awareness of their purpose, they set about abolishing and/or changing, in a gradual process, the existing systems, including their own positions. They explained through the communications media that utopia had come into being in a spirit of true democracy, which meant that each person would be ideally his own government, and that now was the time to bring the ideal into reality, subject, of course, to the agreement of all the people, not just a majority.

The basic principle of each person being his own government implied that there would be no centralisation of government, no laws, no controls; and that all organisations, systems, etc., within the state would be operable under shared arrangements, i.e., that all those involved in an organisation would be, as it were, equal shareholders in it. There were, of course, many existing enterprises in the state which were privately owned. There was no question of any one person or group of people imposing a radical new system on anybody, as, indeed, there was no such thing as a new system, as such, with all its implications of people being asked to behave or conform in specified ways — rather the reverse, since it was the central philosophy of the new state that there would be no interference with individual freedom. What was being promulgated was a new way for people to live and interact together — both as individuals, with total respect for each other's privacy, and as participants in group activities, whatever they might be — without having to cloister themselves off in isolated communities or ashrams, or such-like.

There was a transitional period of about five years while people discussed, through television, radio, newspapers, seminars, etc., how a modern state might operate effectively in a totally democratic way without all the usual institutional trappings and incidental bureaucracies. Being able to manage it in spirit was one thing; achieving it within the restrictiveness of a physical system was something else again. It was no help that commentators from other countries saw what was happening in utopia as either madness or a recipe for total chaos; their more or less unanimous views were that human nature would make the whole idea unworkable.

Nonetheless, as we approach the year 2030 the new utopia is well established with a hundred per cent support, through a referendum, of its citizens. So, now, let's have a look at how it works.

VII

Some people are interested in nature, including farming. Their approach is on the lines of what you call organic farming. They bring their love of nature to bear on the whole operation and all nature responds to them. They produce wonderfully healthy food with an economy of space and effort. Do they own land? Yes, they do. How do they acquire land, if they haven't already got some? By negotiating with somebody who has already got land and arriving at a mutually satisfactory way of exchange (subject, of course, to the owner being willing to sell). Houses, and property generally, change hands in an equally simple manner. There's no need to register ownership, nor are there any legal or taxation costs. Nobody even thinks of cheating or taking what belongs to another.

The inhabitants of utopia continue to use money because it's convenient, in their view, for them to do so. They have highly developed technological aids in order to make daily living easier and to allow people time to expand their own particular fields of interest.

Money is generated in many different ways; for example, through exports to other countries of farm produce (very much in demand because of its remarkable quality); artistic output (e.g., many writers, painters, sculptors, craft workers, movie-makers, photographers, designers, actors, sports stars, musicians, singers, etc.); tourism (the rest of the world becomes increasingly curious about what's happening in utopia in spite of the initial scepticism of commentators); technological and consultancy expertise (past masters at finding ways to short-circuit procedures); industrial aids (some are interested in manufacturing equipment for use in different industries). Internally, there's much exchange of money for products and services.

But, you say, there must be some regulatory systems. How are markets generated abroad? The utopians must have banks, surely? How do people who are unable to work get money? There have to be employers and employees? What about taxation — there has to be, hasn't there?

It's interesting how central a part money plays in people's thoughts when one starts to look at how to create a different way of life on earth; all the questions keep returning to it in some form.

No doubt you will have noticed how dynamic and powerful groups — small, medium, or large — can be when the people in them are on the same wavelength. We know that all the people in utopia are on the same wavelength, even though they have, of course, their own unique and individual ways of expressing their creativity. As I mentioned earlier, they have come on earth in order to serve and to guide humanity, to create a model to show how life on earth can be lived happily. They have not come as miracle workers or to be seen as exempt from the ordinary experiences and limitations of humanity, e.g., illness, ageing. So they are presented with the challenges of being human in the same way as all other humans — although, admittedly, with the advantages of greater awareness and more clearly perceived purpose.

It was obvious to them that money should be seen simply as energy with its place in the overall flow of energy, and that, therefore, it should be taken out of its existing predominant role. Consequently, all banks became redundant (horror of horrors!) in the sense of their traditional functioning — except for what might be called a central bank; also there would be no more taxation.

I have already referred in a general way to agriculture. The farmers, of course, produce food for home consumption as well as for export. They don't have employees. They have advanced technological equipment, and, when necessary, they come together in groups to accomplish certain tasks — a group will help one farmer one day, that farmer will join the group to help another member of the group on a different occasion, and so on. People who may like to experience farm life temporarily are usually facilitated by farmers, who, in turn, get willing helpers — if not always competent ones!

The farmers sell their produce to what I'll call cooperative stores (which, in turn, supply shops and arrange exports — I'll go into that later). The food that they produce satisfies some of their own needs. They use the money that they get from the stores to buy whatever else they require — clothes, equipment, entertainment, etc.

Animals — and, of course, birds — feature very prominently in the state and are much loved. Needless to say, there are no practices such as fox hunting or hare coursing or badger baiting. There's no zoo. Vegetarianism is not a rule (there are no rules) but is widely practised. If animals are killed for the purpose of providing food, it is done with love and respect. There are no slaughterhouses; whatever killing is done is carried out in the animals' own natural habitat. Animals are not exported for slaughter, nor is there any buying or selling of them.

The cooperative stores act as types of clearing houses. As already stated, they supply shops and arrange exports. They are owned and managed by groups of people who are interested in that type of work and each of whom has his own special part to play in the enterprises. They have no hierarchical management structures; those involved act as committees with each member accepting responsibility for a particular area. Some members travel to other countries in connection with marketing of exports, although in general, that's not necessary because the products are so much in demand due to their excellence. The reception and entertainment of trade missions from abroad are the responsibility of designated committee members — who choose that function.

How do the stores get money to pay the farmers and the salaries of their management groups ? From the shops and from the export trade.

There's a wide variety of shops, some very small, some large and some in between. The utopians are generally not much interested in possessions for the sake of possessions. Their houses are tastefully furnished without elaboration — they believe very much in keeping everything as simple as possible. They live comfortably but not ostentatiously. Some of them — particularly the women (surprisingly!) — like jewellery, although most of them seem to wear it sparingly, but to great effect, I would say. They tend to wear clothes that suit their own style and temperament, rather than in response to any fashion trends. Observers or tourists from other countries are often fascinated by the complete lack of uniformity in dress of the utopians; many of the men, as well as the women, are dressed in resplendent colours. There's a great sense of joy and liberation about the way the people wear clothing: incidentally, that also extends to how they dress for business or what might be seen as formal occasions. Their houses, too, reflect their individual styles; even if from the outside there may sometimes be an apparent appearance of uniformity in the construction of the houses, internally they are all arranged in accordance with the wishes of their occupants without any pressure in terms of how they might appear to neighbours or visitors.

The shops are owned and managed by individual families or by larger groups. In so far as the bigger shops are concerned the same system applies as in the case of the cooperative stores, i.e., committees, with each member having his own particular area of responsibility. There's no question of the utopians having decided to adopt an across the board uniform system of running their businesses, but they have found in practice that cooperating with each other on committee or group bases suits them. The committees arrange regular coordinating meetings to overview progress. Money? They get it from their customers.

Is there competition between the shops? Do some of them engage in price cutting in order to attract customers?

Since there are no regulatory laws or rules there are no trading restrictions on shops. It's an entirely open market economy. However, in practice there's no need for competition. People buy what they want where they want to, and they have enough money to do so. The people who manage the shops are not interested in competing with each other — it's not in their nature to be like that. Their real aim is to be happy in their lives, which includes the work they're doing, and to help all others similarly in so far as they can.

There are many hotels in utopia which are becoming increasingly busy because of the expansion in tourism. The hotels are also owned and managed by committees. There is a central tourism committee to coordinate matters affecting the industry generally; the committee also arranges for the issue of passports to those who require them.

VIII

At this stage you may be inclined to ask — what's so different about all this? For example, in a hotel some people will still have to do the routine jobs, such as, reception, cooking, cleaning, waiting at tables, and they can't all be on management committees; even if they were, surely someone would have to allocate functions?

If you think about it, what's happening in utopia isn't, indeed, all that radically different from the trends of your present twentieth century evolution. People are finding increasingly that coming together into groups periodically is significantly helping them spiritually; in other words, they are finding it an effective way to come to terms with, and to feel good about, themselves. The problem is that they still have to survive and for that they need money, which means that somehow money has to be generated. And, in the vast majority of cases, the work that people have to do in order to get money does nothing for them spiritually.

Yes, there are still the routine day to day tasks to be carried out in the utopian hotels (and all their other enterprises) and, even though they take every advantage of their technological aids, there are many jobs that only people can do and that it is important that people should do; for example, the energy that people put into cooking or making beds or waiting at tables is a most influential ingredient in how the people at the receiving end feel.

You may recall that in one of our earlier sessions — in our second book — I intimated that activities haven't relative importance in themselves, that they accrue value because of the effects that they have on the performers. The utopians are at a level of awareness where they understand that principle. They are there to serve humanity, but they are not there as menials working long hours for meagre wages. They are there in their own right as co-owners of the enterprises with which they happen to be involved (co-creators of the universe). So all the people who run each hotel, large or small, have each got equal shares in the ownership of the hotel. Tasks are allocated by choice and are, of course, subject to rotation, if people so wish. There's never any difficulty about demarcation of work; the accountant today could be peeling potatoes next year — but people's aptitudes and wishes are taken into account so that nobody is ever compelled to perform work that they find repellent to them. In fact, that couldn't arise anyway — who would do the compelling?

What's happening in utopia is that the people have brought into the workplaces the spirit, the unity of purpose and the enjoyment that you may see operating in voluntary groupings at present — and, of course, most important — the opportunities and the environment have been created to allow them to do that.

I need hardly go into detail about the other utopian enterprises, such as manufacturing industries. By choice, they are all operated on the same principle — co-ownership, with all the workers forming committees of management. If you're thinking that this arrangement could entail very unwieldy committees, it doesn't — they split up into sub-committees, as considered desirable.

Doesn't the central principle of each utopian being his own government conflict with the seemingly uniform committee system which appears like a form of decentralised government? No, there's no conflict. As I have said earlier, each person has complete freedom about what type of work he will do or, indeed, whether to do any work at all (although that doesn't happen, except through illness or old age or incapacity of some kind). There's no unemployment, even if that means that some people work shorter hours. Nobody is ever sacked or compulsorily retired; people make their own choices as to whether or how long they stay in particular jobs. Nobody imposes standard work practices on anybody — each person works to his own style and has unlimited scope as to how he fulfils his role. Individuals come together in common endeavour without sacrificing their individuality in any way.

IX

I still haven't dealt in detail with the big question of money and how it is managed.

All the various enterprises — agriculture, shops, industries, hotels, entertainment, etc. — generate their own incomes. They each give a tenth of their total incomes to the central bank (which is also managed by a committee of co-owners!) and they share the rest equally amongst their members. If this arrangement causes headaches to any particular enterprise (although that doesn't happen) it is open to it to give a smaller contribution, or none at all. (Even to say that is misleading, however, because there's no form of compulsion or mandatory requirement). If an enterprise is still in difficulty (which, again, is only a theoretical situation) it can get financial relief from the central bank — not as a loan, but as a grant.

Apart from being there as a safeguard against any financial problems in the different enterprises in the state, the central bank deals with arrangements about foreign currencies. It may also help, if the need arises, where public services, such as transport or health, are concerned. In addition, it has a special fund set aside to help any individuals who for some reason may not be able to work, or whose circumstances place financial burdens on them; all that they have to do is to ask for whatever income they feel they need and that will be made available to them. (That's what your governments do to you through imposed systems of taxation; the utopians have neatly given their power back to the people.) Should there be any difficulty about the fund not being adequate at any time to meet the requests for help (there hasn't been) all the bank need do is ask for public subscriptions, which would be readily forthcoming. (It may seem strange that people are automatically given what they feel they need, but there would never be any question of utopians asking for more — or less — than that.)

X

In the modern world, and, of course, particularly in cities, the provision and regulation of transport are perennial problems. How do the utopians solve those problems without imposing any regulations?

Their solution is basically very simple. The fact that there are no centralised establishments, e.g., governments, (apart from the central bank), is a help towards having a fairly even spread of population throughout the state; nevertheless, there's still quite a heavy concentration of people in the cities. People don't bring their cars into the cities at all. This has happened entirely of their own volition. Some people take their cars occasionally to the outskirts of the cities to within walking distance of where they want to go. Different groups and/or individuals operate buses and coaches and taxicabs (again, needless to say, on a shared ownership basis, where applicable) and, because there is such free movement within the cities, there are no traffic jams and travel is a speedy and pleasant experience. Small flying machines — somewhat on the style of helicopters, but more advanced in design — are popular, and becoming more so; some utopians are concentrating on developing more sophisticated technological methods of flying so that the vast open air space can be utilised more efficiently for the benefit of the people (and without encroaching too much on birds' territory!).

There are also, of course, aeroplanes and trains (managed on the usual basis). There's no competition between the different groupings since nobody is obsessed with making money and nobody is short of money; the primary motivation is to provide efficient service and to do so cheerfully.

There are some small hospitals, but because the people are living their lives in such relaxed and harmonious ways they are generally in good health. Many of them like to meditate regularly by themselves and/or with groups. They are most attentive to preserving the serenity of their inner being, and that's reflected in their outer expression. Their countenances are open and friendly, and their smiles light up their eyes. Their doctors and nurses have studied and developed what are known as alternative or complementary healing techniques as well as what might be called orthodox medicine. Their services, both as teachers and as healers, are increasingly in demand in other countries, so that they are often absent from home for long periods. That's their own choice, of course.

Since there's no longer any formal government, how is utopia represented in relation to other countries, e.g., embassies, visits by heads of state? Once again, through a committee system.

Because the utopians don't have rulers there's nobody in a position, or charged with responsibility, to decide who will perform what function — or, indeed, whether there's a function to be performed at all. People naturally gravitate towards their areas of interest and take whatever initiatives, and make whatever responses, they think are needed. Everything is done, every position is filled, by agreement. Understandably, this may seem like a haphazard and impractical way of ordering affairs of state. But isn't it essentially what democracy means? In any case, the utopians had already designed in spirit before they came into earth the broad outline of what their roles were going to be in this new exploration in consciousness. Colleagues in spirit, who are not incarnating, are guiding them, so that the density of the earth vibration will not cloud their insight and interfere with their overall purpose.

I think I have said enough about the arrangements by which the state is managed for you to get the general picture.

XI

The utopians do not, in practice, have formal religious belief systems, although, of course, as is the case in spirit, there is complete freedom of religious expression. As I have already explained, they accept their own divinity in their humanness and they are at one with God in them. To them God is not an external force to be worshipped but, rather, the centre of their own being continually expressed both in themselves and in everybody and everything around them. They have come to unite, not to divide, and to help people to find that pot of gold at the end of the rainbow for which they are endlessly searching and which, of course, is reunion with God in them.

There are church buildings in utopia which people use for group discussions, adventures in spirit, meditations, talks etc., as well as religious ceremonies, if desired. Some people like to savour the atmosphere and the peace of empty churches.

The utopians are fun loving people. They love music, singing, dancing, parties, etc., according to their individual tastes. They have theatres, concert halls, cinemas, dance halls, sporting arenas, etc., which cater for varying interests (highbrow to lowbrow!). Some of them enjoy alcohol — and occasionally over-indulge, with predictable effects! They don't use drugs, other than for medicinal purposes.

Utopians are not sexually promiscuous, since to them sexuality is linked to creative expression and intimacy. They enjoy their sexuality and they express it in all their activities. Because their work is satisfying, enjoyable and fulfilling no part of their creativity is suppressed.

There is no formal institution of marriage in utopia — in keeping with their ways of having no formalities of any kind; and, of course, they are manifesting on earth as in spirit. Before they were born into physical bodies they had made arrangements with their soul mates that they would meet and share sexual intimacy within the material sphere. They have created family situations, they have their own houses or apartments, their own private worlds to the extent that they wish, some of them have children (who will usually have come from the second rather than the fourth stage but are ready to move beyond the second stage).

You will probably have noticed that in the evolution of the twentieth century sexual expression has moved through phases of prudishness to what was known as free love — which was facilitated by the development of contraception. Sex qua sex became an end in itself. As the end of the century approached, however, it became more and more evident that many people wanted more than merely mechanical or physical sexual release; they were looking for an intimacy of communication as an integral ingredient in sexual intercourse. Women, for whom the century had brought more freedom in the acknowledgment of their sexuality, have been at the forefront of the acceleration in the movement of consciousness, and in the process many of them have found gaps opening up between themselves and their partners, if married or in such-like relationships, or between themselves, if they are heterosexual, and men generally, because men on the whole tended to be slower to move beyond purely rational or conditioned perspectives. So, as the twentieth century drew to a close, the search for intimacy became more pronounced and the need for a new language or different communication in sexuality grew deeper.

In the utopia of 2030 the people are used to sexual intimacy. They enjoy sexual union uninhibitedly. They have no special interest in techniques, other than whatever is mutually pleasing. Needless to say, their bodies are never occasions of shame to them. As I have already said, they are not sexually promiscuous, not due to any conditioned morality but because they don't believe that sexual intimacy can be achieved in that way.

They welcome children because they like them and also because it's an important part of their purpose that they are vehicles for souls to experience — or re-experience — physical life as a means of growing in consciousness. Before coming to earth they will have made arrangements with the souls who will be born to them as children (and their guides) and these arrangements determine the number of children born to each couple. Some will have made no arrangements about having children, and some will have chosen to have sexual intimacy with partners of their own gender. You understand that they see sexual expression as a means of helping intimacy of communication rather than in any mould of morality.

They make no moral judgements about contraception or abortion. They know that if they have made arrangements with souls to be born to them as children those souls will be sure to come to them at the appropriate times; they trust that they will respond to the signals.

Children are much loved and are usually reared by their parents in their own homes. They are not given any specific religious training but they are imbued with the deep spirituality of their parents and teachers. They are aware of, and consciously communicate with, their guides/guardian angels, and they are also, at an early stage in their lives, helped by their parents to be aware of feelings of connectedness or unity with God in them.

Education is geared very much to individual preferences. Arrangements are made for children to be brought together (on a co-educational basis) where they are taught by those who have chosen to do that work. There are no set methods of teaching, no competitive examinations; from an early age children are given opportunities to find and develop their own unique talents.

There's no peer group pressure nor is there any bar to possibilities for higher or expanded education. There are no requirements for formal quali-fications, such as certificates, or diplomas, or degrees. The people are high-ly proficient and knowledgeable within their chosen fields — which include all known forms of human expression, as well as some pioneering ones. Learning is a constantly joyful experience. Career guidance presents no difficulties because creativity is never suppressed and there are always either existing openings for employment in a person's selected field or he can easily create one — he will be both encouraged and helped to do so.

The utopian system (or no system) of education has become the envy of many observers and the practice has grown of sending children and young adults from other countries to be trained by the utopian teachers. This is a development which is greatly welcomed in utopia and which is, of course, very much in line with the purpose of its existence. In due course the for-eign students will, if they wish to do so, introduce aspects of the utopian ways into their own systems.

XII

Utopia has no army, no navy, no courts, no prisons, no police force. So is it open house for invaders or robbers or lawlessness of whatever form? In your physical world, as it exists at present, there's a huge emphasis on security in all aspects of life, including personal safety, private property and national boundaries. In spirit there's obviously no need for any of that. So the issue of security presents a forceful (!) challenge to adventuring souls who wish to merge to an advanced extent the physical and spirit worlds.

In utopia itself, because of the people's level of awareness, there's no need for any security system since there is total respect for each person's being. Nobody would even think of imposing on another, or encroaching on another person's space, or taking what belongs to somebody else. But what's to stop another country invading utopia, or people from other places coming to rob and plunder, since there would be no physical preventative measures, apparently?

You may remember that in a previous session I talked about how guides can keep your aura clear if you ask them to do so. I went on to explain that the way in which they do that is rather like an electric fence being placed around your aura so that any 'invader' would experience something of a shock in trying to get through. The auras of the utopians are all protected in that way and the concentrated power of their positivity embraces the whole country. Any invaders with negative intentions would find themselves up against an intangible force which would be all the more effective because of not being visible nor, indeed, perhaps, understandable or explainable within the rationale of human conditioning. Yet it is true that utopia experiences no invasions of any kind, either private or national, nor does it anticipate any.

Here it is, I think, relevant to observe how what happens internally reflects itself externally. A person who lacks self-acceptance, which, in the final analysis, is due to separation from God, finds it necessary to try to create inner security by presenting a defensive mask to the world. The emphasis on external security systems is a projection of people's inner being.

XIII

Some people from other countries wish to go to live in utopia. Usually, they are people who are in tune in themselves with the utopian way and fit easily into the new lifestyle. There are no difficulties of overcrowding or overpopulation.

The communications media — newspapers, television, radio — play important roles in utopia. They are free to print or broadcast anything they like since there are no controls. That's also true, of course, where publications of any kind are concerned, such as, books, magazines, videos, tapes. They place great emphasis on expressing their creativity in whatever form it comes and they are usually very willing to share the fruits of that creativity with others. They don't go in for pornography in their literature or visual presentations, not from a moralistic standpoint but because they don't enjoy it. They don't isolate themselves from the rest of the world in any way and generally they keep themselves well informed through the media about what's happening world-wide. People who are interested in communications have extensive scope for expressing themselves; anybody who wants to is free to publish his own newspaper, magazine, etc., or to set up his own television or radio station. In practice, all of these ventures are undertaken by co-operative effort (with, of course, co-ownership).

Utopia inherited telephone and postal systems from the previous administrations. In line with what happens generally in the new state, routine operations are largely automated and the systems as a whole are overseen by committees who manage and co-own them. The users pay annual rental charges for both services, the rates of which (modest) are determined by the committees, and there are no charges for telephone calls or postage stamps or any of the telecommunications or postal services provided. The post offices which were already in place have continued to be used for the reception and distribution of mail and also as collection points for any money which people receive from the central bank. Each post office makes its own arrangements with the bank.

XIV

All administrative procedures in utopia are simple, with no "red tape", no form filling. There is real democracy because the people cooperate with each other in a spirit of total harmony and nobody is seeking to control anybody else, or to be protected from anybody else. The people are secure in themselves individually and that inner feeling spreads outwards and creates the environment in which they live.

Because all the governmental and other institutional arrangements no longer exist, many people whose energies would formerly have been occupied in such employments as the civil service, courts, police, prisons, banks, insurance offices, were set free to express their creativity in ways which would reflect more truly their own personalities and styles. There are no "square pegs in round holes" in utopia. The state is not burdened with heavy administrative costs, which releases money for more creative purposes.

XV

Perhaps the thought enters your head that the picture I have been painting of a country which is all serenity and harmony and simplicity is one of unrelieved dullness? Where's the "buzz" that can be got from conflict, argumentation, juicy bits of gossip?

Those questions are, of course, as relevant to life in spirit ("heaven") as they are to life in our earthly utopia. The fact is that as souls regain their lost awareness their inner harmony increases. It's fair to say — isn't it? — that people generally don't like to live in states of conflict. Usually, great stress is involved for people who are forced for one reason or another to live in discordant atmospheres. People who enjoy looking at films showing battles or wars don't want to be participants in such martial escapades. Equally, people who flock to see a play featuring dramatic conflicts in personal relationships don't want to have similar conflicts in their own lives. Or people who avidly read thrillers which involve murders, or victimisations of different kinds, can become totally absorbed in the stories because they know that they don't have to relate to them in real life. Or people can savour the cut and thrust of courtroom exchanges, although they would themselves shrink from such experiences in their own lives.

What happens as awareness increases is that people, if they wish, can enjoy conflict without having to experience it — for example, in movies, plays, books, sports (!). They can have the fun of participation without its pain. They can also participate, e.g., in sports, as much as they like, in the consciousness that they're playing games. They don't become namby pambies, they glow more in their being, they express themselves more openly and more vividly, they don't automatically agree with each other for the sake of agreement or compromise, they may, indeed, hold totally differing points of view on certain issues and strongly voice their opinions but without resentment, or defensiveness, or dogmatism, or seeking to impose their ideas in any way; in other words, what I'm trying to say is that they enjoy themselves thoroughly.

XVI

The question on which this chapter was based was — what is life going to be like on planet earth in the future? I have attempted to answer the question by using an illustration of a new country which could serve as a model for the planet as a whole in a gradually evolving process. I have tried to give you an outline with some, but not too much, detail.

Since it is true that we are all spirit beings, some of us temporarily in physical bodies and some of us not confined in that way, it is fitting, I think, that we should seek to understand each other better. So I have endeavoured to bridge the gap between our worlds by making, I hope, the world of spirit more real for you and easier to imagine. It is difficult to convey by description, which necessarily defines, the joy of life in spirit, particularly at the fourth stage and beyond. I hope we have succeeded, to some extent, at least.

Is utopia a possibility, not just for a small section, but for all of the planet? Yes. It will obviously take a long time in your terms and it will inevitably happen gradually, but that it will happen I have no doubt. Then planet earth will have fulfilled its purpose as a vehicle for regaining lost awareness and will truly be a divine playground.

Conclusion

15th January: The aim of this book has been to move us further along the way of merging the spirit and physical worlds. In particular, the final long chapter is an attempt to create a deeper understanding of life and all its potential, as well as to eliminate at least some of the controlling influences that have strangled so much of the adventuresome, exploratory, spirit which is present, but too often suppressed, in all people.

I know that many people (particularly those who won't — at present — be interested in reading this book) would immediately dismiss the utopian way of life that I have described as totally unrealistic. Yet, already, millions of people throughout the world are moving in that direction, but feeling that they have to get away from existing controlling systems, or to live with them without fulfilment. I'm not seeking to present you with a pipe dream. It is all eminently practical, with people's energies being used freely and constructively rather than defensively and often destructively.

We started this book on a note of joyful welcome and love. We are concluding it in a spirit of loving continuity and hope filled certainty, wishing you all the early achievement of the utopia of your dreams.

Transformation

Eight butterflies
Spreading gentle wings as a carpet
Across the ghostly path
Of memory.
Caterpillars once,
Carrying within themselves the radiance
Of profligate beauty
Fluttering along the stream
Of awakening consciousness.
A past
Painful in its crawling conditioning
Of seeping shame
Undermining the wonder
Of a fairyland
Rivered on the edge of nowhere;
Yet seeded by its mystic power into
A present
Glorious in its vision
Of being; forever free,
Coming out from under the leaves
Of its self-imposed prison
And revealing itself
For what it is.
The earthbound unlovely caterpillar
Becomes the gorgeous ungravitied butterfly.
The transformation is beyond effort.

PMcM

~ ~ ~ ~

Appendix

The Cathar Prophecy of 1244 A.D. : that the church of love would be proclaimed in 1986

It has no fabric, only understanding.

It has no membership save those who know they belong.

It has no rivals, because it is non-competitive.

It has no ambition, because it seeks only to serve.

It knows no boundaries for nationalisms are unloving.

It is not of itself, because it seeks to enrich all groups and religions.

It acknowledges all great teachers of all the ages who have shown the truth of love.

Those who participate practise the truth of love in all their beings.

There is no walk of life or nationality that is a barrier.

Those who are, know.

It seeks not to teach, but to be, and, by being, enrich.

It recognises that the way we are may be the way of those around us because we are that way.

It recognises the whole planet as a being of which we are a part.

It recognises that the time has come for the supreme transmutation, the ultimate alchemical act of conscious change of the ego into a voluntary return to the Whole.

It does not proclaim itself with a loud voice but in the subtle realms of loving.

It salutes all those in the past who have blazened the path but have paid the price.

It admits no hierarchy or structure, for no one is greater than another.

Its members shall know each other by their deeds and being and by their eyes, and by no other outward sign save the fraternal embrace.

Each one will dedicate their life to the silent loving of their neighbour, the environment, and the planet, whilst carrying out their task, however exalted or humble.

It recognises the supremacy of the great idea which may only be accomplished if the human race practises the supremacy of love.

It has no reward to offer either here or in the hereafter save that of the ineffable joy of being and loving.

Each shall seek to advance the cause of understanding, doing good by stealth, and teaching only by example.

They shall heal their neighbour, their community and our planet.

They shall know no fear and feel no shame, and their witness shall prevail over all odds.

It has no secret, or arcanus, no initiation save that of true understanding of the power of love and that, if we want it to be so, the world will change, but only if we change ourselves first.

All those who belong, belong, they belong to the church of love.

~ ~ ~ ~